Shared
Vulnerability

Shared_____
Vulnerability
THE MEDIA AND
AMERICAN PERCEPTIONS OF
THE BHOPAL DISASTER

LEE WILKINS

CONTRIBUTIONS TO THE STUDY OF
MASS MEDIA AND COMMUNICATIONS,
——————————————— NUMBER 8

Greenwood Press
New York • Westport, Connecticut • London

Library of Congress Cataloging-in-Publication Data

Wilkins, Lee.
    Shared vulnerability.

    (Contributions to the study of mass media and
communications, ISSN 0732-4456 ; no. 8)
    Bibliography: p.
    Includes index.
    1. Disasters in the press—United States.
2. Bhopal Union Carbide Plant Disaster, Bhopal, India,
1984—Public opinion   3. Public opinion—United States. I. Title.   II. Series.
PN4888.D57W5   1987   070.4'493631'79   86-25838
ISBN 0-313-25265-3 (lib. bdg. : alk. paper)

Library of Congress Catalog Card Number: 86-25838
ISBN: 0-313-25265-3
ISSN: 0732-4456

First published in 1987

Greenwood Press, Inc.
88 Post Road West, Westport, Connecticut 06881

Printed in the United States of America

The paper used in this book complies with the
Permanent Paper Standard issued by the National
Information Standards Organization (Z39.48-1984).

10   9   8   7   6   5   4   3   2   1

Copyright Acknowledgment

We gratefully acknowledge WIDE WORLD PHOTOS for permission to use the
photographs that follow Chapter 3.

For David

Contents

Illustrations

Preface

The research outlined in this book is based on two convictions.
First, technological hazards are created by human beings and
hence can be mitigated by human beings; and second, the mass
media have a central role to play in societal discussion of ways
to blunt the potential harmful impact of otherwise useful technologies. The tragedy of Bhopal is merely a symptom of a worldwide industrial disease, one which has plagued humanity since
the beginnings of the industrial revolution. Bhopal is the latest
evolution in the plight of the working poor so eloquently described by Charles Dickens or the statistics Karl Marx unearthed
in his research in Britain that led to the writing of *Das Kapital*.
In both cases, individuals—with distinct points of view—expressed horror at what the promise of the industrial revolution
had become. Bhopal, too, causes such a gasp of horror, not only
because of the lingering death and injury but also, in a deeper
sense, because the Bhopal plant and the pesticides it manufac-
tured promised the opposite of what the event has come to
represent.

Because of the premises underlying the research, this two-
pronged study of the media coverage of the Bhopal disaster will
interest scholars, students and government officials in a variety
of disciplines and roles. Mass communication scholars, who seek
to understand how the media portray significant events and to
learn what it is that audiences retain from those portrayals, will
be interested in the study because it is one of few which analyzes

both segments of the message—audience relationship while focusing on a single event. In addition, those mass communication scholars who study coverage of science and technology will find media coverage of science-related stories is more than merely the sum of the facts produced and the sources cited. The mass media, without collective or conscious intent, are contributing to a mythology about science which may have some central implications for democratic decision making.

Those scholars, primarily in the disciplines of geography and sociology, whose work focuses on issues of hazard mitigation will find the study informative for the portrait it paints of what some have termed the "mass mediated" reality. The study reveals, for example, how traditional definitions of news and traditional newsgathering practices result in hazard coverage which is event–centered, thus avoiding long–range questions of planning and resource allocation which play a significant role in mitigating the impact of both natural and technological hazards. While the volume is critical of such coverage, those who seek to mitigate hazard impact have historically placed enormous reliance on the mass media to inform the public about certain aspects of various events. The insights in this study may provide both scholars and government officials whose goal is hazard mitigation with specifics they can use to educate the public and journalists about hazards plus some specific strategies for doing so. The issue thus becomes how to allow journalists, government officials and hazards scholars to work together to promote public debate which will lead to decisions to promote hazard mitigation.

Finally, political scientists will be interested in the work for the normative theoretical questions it raises about the role of the mass media in a democracy. Individual feelings of helplessness about hazards—and memories of news accounts which emphasize those feelings—raise some central questions about the role of public opinion and public opinion formation on particular issues. The book does not attempt to answer all these questions, but rather to provide a framework which will allow more informed scholarly debate on these issues.

There are, as well, some things this book is not. It is not a condemnation of science, technology, Union Carbide, the American or Indian governments or the mass media. It seems to me there is both blame and praise enough to share. My view remains that the issue which most needs to be explored, in both a scholarly and a pragmatic sense, is not what went wrong but rather how society and its component individuals and institutions can take this one event and learn from it. My goal in engaging in this research is one I believe I share with both journalists and those concerned with hazard mitigation: preventing more Bhopals. Having agreed on such a goal, the issue for me then becomes how can we, in a democratic society, achieve it. I hope this book will be one step in that direction.

There are some textual notes. The research outlined in the book, which was funded by the National Science Foundation, may be divided into two parts: a content analysis of media coverage of the first two months of the Bhopal disaster, and the report of public opinion polls designed to discover what Americans remembered of the event and of media reports. Chapter 2 provides the scholarly and methodological framework for the research. The content analysis—as well as its theoretical implications—is described in Chapters 3, 4 and 5 while the results of the public opinion surveys, and their theoretical implications, are outlined in Chapter 6. Chapter 7 focuses on the ethical implications of media coverage of the event, while Chapter 8 includes a four-part plan for improving media coverage of such events. References in the various chapters refer to bibliographic entries; endnotes have been used when specific stories included in the study are cited in the text.

While the overall tone of the work is scholarly, I have tried to write it in such a way that the significant findings will be understandable to—and certainly debatable by—professional journalists and government officials. It is my belief that only through dialogue between various segments of society, in this case scholars, the working press and various government and corporate representatives, can we begin the collective and important work of hazard mitigation.

Acknowledgments

Disasters are generally considered collaborative efforts, and this book—disaster or not—certainly qualifies as one.

This research would not have been possible without the guidance and support provided by Dr. William Anderson at the National Science Foundation, who believed in the project and was willing to trust a fledgling scholar. The grant proposal he approved, in turn, would not have been possible without the support and guidance from two of my colleagues at the University of Colorado: Associate Vice–Chancellor Risa Palm and Dean Russell E. Shain. Their contributions, both to the idea for the project and to the writing of this book, have been invaluable.

Six graduate students worked many hours for low pay coding the news stories and public opinion surveys which are the base of this study. Marcia Jarmel, John Wilkens, Bonnie Darnell, Mark Herlinger, Mary George and Laura Caruso contributed much enthusiasm and insight to the project. The news stories were collected with the help of David Hall, editor, the *Denver Post*, who allowed me to use the paper's Nexus terminal. The data itself could never have been analyzed without help from Arthur McFarland, Dr. Gary McClelland and Dr. Stephen B. Jones, all at the University of Colorado. My colleagues in the Environment and Behavior Program, a part of the Institute for Behavioral Science—William Riebsame and Gilbert White—contributed a supportive environment. Dr. E. L. Quarantelli, of the Disaster Research Center, Dr. Jay Black, Utah State University, and Dr.

James C. Davies, University of Oregon, read early drafts of portions of the manuscript and were generous with their comments. Beth Conny, University of Colorado, and Philip Patterson, Oklahoma Christian College, helped with both editing and overall evaluation. J. Roy Bardsley, of Bardsley and Haslacher in Portland, Oregon, provided polling expertise, and Wil Lepkowski, senior editor for *Chemical and Engineering News*, was generous with his time and insight.

Dr. James T. Sabin and Mary R. Sive, my editors at Greenwood Press, supported the book from initial proposal onward, and Judy Strong typed the manuscript with her usual patience and good will.

My biggest debt, however, is to my family. My parents, Tom and Carrie, provided support for work my father politely labeled esoteric. My daughter, Miranda, managed to make a harmonious transition through the terrible twos, leaving her mother able to write coherently some days. And my husband David, the geography major, understood hazards well before I did. Not only did he read early drafts of the manuscript, but he provided the support I needed most, oblivious to the hazards of marrying a college professor. It is because of him that this book was completed, and it is to him that this book is dedicated.

Shared
Vulnerability

1

The Year of Bhopal

THE CULTURE OF TECHNOLOGICAL HAZARD

Like many tragedies in human history, the Bhopal, India, disaster began with a relatively innocuous request. At about 9:30 p.m. on December 2, 1984, a supervisor, despite safety regulations, asked a novice worker at the chemical plant to wash out a pipe with water. The employee complied, not realizing a drain in the area was improperly closed. The water from the cleanup seeped into a partially buried tank, No. 610, containing methyl isocyanate (MIC), a chemical base for a number of insecticides, the most well known of which is Sevin. In final form, Sevin is easily biodegradable and considered an environmentally safe pesticide. But its MIC component is highly volatile in the presence of water. So, as the water seeped into the tank, a chain reaction began. About 40 tons of the liquid began to heat up, and the pressure began to build.[1]

The chemical convulsion, however, was merely one of the pressures focusing on the Bhopal plant and, to a lesser extent, the chemical industry in much of the Third World. With encouragement from the Indian government, Union Carbide opened the Bhopal plant in 1977. While the company sought to increase profits at home, India viewed the Bhopal facility as a symbol of development. Historically the subcontinent had been unable to feed itself. But, with the aid of modern agricultural techniques, including the use of pesticides like Sevin, by the mid–1970s India had become a net grain exporter. The Union Carbide plant also provided jobs; in fact, the Indian government waived statutory Indian-ownership requirements to obtain the facility. Ownership of the Bhopal plant was vested in Union Carbide of India, Ltd., which controlled 50.1 percent of the facility, while the remainder was held by the parent American corporation. To provide even more jobs, the Indian government required the Bhopal plant be labor intensive. Thus the Indian facility, while resembling a similar Union Carbide plant in Institute, West Virginia, lacked computerized safety systems. Human labor took their place. And, because the plant—originally built on the outskirts of the city of 900,000—did provide jobs, slums mushroomed around it, first in defiance of local regulations but later with the acquiescence of Indian planners who realized it was futile to try to regulate centuries-old living patterns.

There were economic pressures as well. The 1970s, a decade of global inflation and diminishing corporate profits, also began to squeeze the facility. In the two years preceding the accident the plant had been losing money. Highly trained staff members were laid off, and workers with less training were hired in their places. Some jobs remained vacant. Morale declined. The plant was put up for sale.

"The whole industrial culture of Union Carbide at Bhopal went down the drain," Kamal Pareek, a former Bhopal project engineer who resigned in December 1983, disheartened with developments at the plant, told the *New York Times*.[2] "Maintenance practices became poor, and things generally got sloppy. The plant didn't seem to have a future, and a lot of skilled people became depressed and left as a result."

There were some warnings. A 1982 inspection by a team from the parent American firm found a number of safety problems representing "a higher potential for a serious accident or more serious consequences if an accident should occur."[3] Many of the problems detailed in the 1982 report were corrected—but not all. The Bhopal plant also had been the site of several accidents, including one fatality in 1981 when a worker died as a result of exposure of phosgene—the World War I mustard gas which is a component of MIC. About six months before the accident, an

Indian journalist warned that the plant was ripe for catastrophe. His reports received limited circulation in India and no coverage in the United States.

So the pressures continued. A twelve-person maintenance crew was replaced by a team of six—including the novice worker who was asked to clean out the pipe. Unreliable gauges and valves were not inspected or replaced. On October 22, the scrubber, which was designed to neutralize any gas escaping into the atmosphere from the plant, was shut down for repairs, despite company safety regulations which insisted on its continuous operation. Six days before the accident, the refrigeration unit on the MIC tank, which maintained the chemical at temperatures less conducive to a runaway reaction, was shut down—again for repairs. About an hour after the worker had completed his chore, another worker noticed that the pressure gauge on the MIC tank was registering about five times normal. He thought nothing of it; the gauge had been unreliable. And, at about 11:30 that Sunday night, when a yellowish fog caused the eyes of workers inside the plant to begin to burn and sting, the supervisor decided it was no real emergency. He would deal with the problem after tea.

By then it was too late.

Forces, both internal and external, converged. Some of the MIC stored in tank No. 610 began to vaporize—and tank No. 610 was full because workers had been unable to empty it. The vaporizing chemical continued to infiltrate the plant and, simultaneously, the runaway chemical reaction, unchecked by the refrigeration unit, intensified. The pressure in the tank became so enormous the tank itself eventually cracked. The gas spewed past the only safety system still in operation—a water spray designed to neutralize escaping gas. But the enormous pressures forced the gas to vent above the spray valve. Raising the valve was one of the 1982 safety recommendations which had not been followed. The yellow fog raced through the broken scrubber and out into the atmosphere where the prevailing winds carried it toward the nearby slums.

The workers inside the facility, who were untrained for such an emergency, panicked. They ran, making sure they traveled across the wind. The slum residents, most of whom were asleep, were not so lucky. As the fog settled to earth, many awoke with tearing eyes and burning sensations in their chests. The wind currents scattered the gas—it skittered down some alleys and streets and left others untouched. Some died in their sleep. Others ran, some of them toward the plant which, about two hours after the leak began, sounded an alarm. They ran to help the facility which in the local Hindu dialect, *kheti ki dawai*, made "medicine for crops."[4] Some saved their own lives; others churned into the path of the gas. The old and the young were most vulnerable. All had become unwilling participants—as many as 2,500 dead and 200,000 injured—in the worst industrial accident in human history.[5]

The Immediate Aftermath

Bhopal residents unaffected by the gas awoke to find government offices, schools, markets and shops closed for the day. Chief Minister Arjun Singh authorized the arrest of four plant officials—the assistant works manager, the production manager, the plant supervisor and another supervisor, all Indian nationals—in connection with the leak. The United News of India erroneously reported the deadly gas was methyl iso cyanide, adding to the confusion about MIC and its toxic properties. Doctors, who were treating hundreds of victims throughout the city, complained they could not obtain adequate information about the chemical's toxicity. The state government approved payment equal to $500 to the families of those killed in the disaster and $100 to families of those hospitalized. It also declared the following day, Tuesday, a day of mourning.

In the United States, Union Carbide halted production of MIC at its Institute plant and sent a doctor and four technicians to Bhopal to aid the relief effort.

Medical aid was needed. The next day, two Bhopal doctors said the death toll from the gas would reach at least 1,000, despite the Indian government's much lower reports. Rumors of another leak spread through the city, causing some panic, and doctors and hospitals continued to be overwhelmed by the victims.

Back in the United States, Union Carbide Chairman Warren Anderson said it would take from two to three weeks to determine the cause of the accident. Anderson said he believed it was his job "at this moment to make sure that whatever suffering occurred can be minimized."[6]

Corporate spokesman Jackson Browning told American reporters that a filter—the vent scrubber—should have served as a safety device, but corporate officials in the United States did not know why it failed.

Official evaluations of MIC began to surface. The Occupational Safety and Health Administration (OSHA) reported the chemical is dangerous when diluted to twenty parts per million, and U.S. workers may not be exposed to more than .02 parts per million in an eight-hour day. Medical experts said high concentrations of the gas can lead to pulmonary edema—fluid accumulation in the lungs—coughing, tears, chest pains and difficult breathing.

The first pictures of the Bhopal tragedy reached America through the three news networks on December 4. Each rated Bhopal the top story of the day.

Vivid word portraits of Bhopal also emerged in the American print media.

> Daya Ram carries his dead year-old son covered with a red towel to the smoking cremation grounds. Young Sanaz Bee and Abram Kahn mourn their father and mother. Everywhere the survivors and the dead are side by side. The blind lead the blind [an Associated Press reporter wrote].
>
> Thousands of dead cattle lie bloated in the streets and pastures, so babies cry for milk. The leaves on the trees are yellow and shriveled. The turnips and spinach are chemically scorched and covered by fine white film. Ponds are discolored.
>
> The stench of death hangs over Bhopal, mingled with the smoke of mass funeral pyres from what workers are calling "devil night." Gravediggers open mass trenches. Tailors are stitching shrouds. Doctors are struggling to prevent a second tragedy: an epidemic.[7]

By December 5, doctors in Bhopal had a new worry: the spread of disease through corpses. The official death toll had reached 1,250 to 1,400, and an additional 50,000 residents had been treated for injuries. The Indian minister for chemicals and fertilizer, Vasant Sathe, said he expected victim compensation according to American standards. He also accused Union Carbide of failing to provide safety devices in the Bhopal plant.

The same day in Institute, West Virginia, the community planning committee asked Union Carbide to install a better warning system at the Institute plant, which employed about 1,400 people. The corporation, in turn, denied Indian allegations about safety devices and standards, and said it might shut down its Woodbine, Georgia, plant after the supply of MIC at the facility had been converted into pesticide.

On December 6 news agencies quoted United Nations officials, who asked to remain anonymous, as saying many Third World countries remain poorly equipped to manage and protect their environments.

In India, the official death toll reached 1,600. The same day Carbide Chairman Anderson and five other corporate officials flew to Bhopal, but were denied admission to the plant. Instead, Anderson was placed under house arrest and charged with negligence and criminal liability in connection with the leak.

Doctors reported eight stillbirths after the leak and said traces of phosgene and cyanate were being found in bodies. About 500 Bhopal residents marched on the home of Chief Minister Singh to protest inadequate victim relief.

And, because the event itself had begun to have international repercussions, Prime Minister Rajiv Gandhi released a condolence letter from President Ronald Reagan, who wrote, "The tragic incident that occurred at Bhopal has shocked the American nation. Our hearts go out to those who suffer."[8]

While Bhopal and its residents struggled to return to normal, Americans began to engage in a different sort of damage control. West Virginia Governor Jay Rockefeller ordered the state Air Pollution Control Commission to keep a twenty-four hour watch on the Institute plant. Union Carbide stock fell more than five points on the New York Stock Exchange. The company, the third largest chemical manufacturer in the United States and the nation's thirty-seventh largest corporation, denied it was seeking financial protection under U.S. bankruptcy laws.

There were reactions in other nations as well. In West Germany one of two gasoline bombs inside a Union Carbide plant at Milstead exploded. There were no injuries or deaths, and the words "Poison Killers" and "Swine" were found spray painted on the walls.

In Rio de Janeiro, Brazilian officials blocked the unloading of a shipment of MIC at the port.

On December 7 Indian authorities, after some intervention of U.S. embassy personnel and possibly the White House, released Anderson, who was taken to the Bhopal airport and then to New Delhi. Singh explained Anderson's arrest, saying, "We are convinced on the basis of facts already available that each of them have criminal liability for the events that led to the grave tragedy."[9]

Meanwhile, shops in Bhopal had begun to reopen, and survivors had started to return home. The official death toll was placed at 1,600 with 200,000 injured.

In the United States, the first of what would become a flood of lawsuits against Union Carbide was filed in U.S. District Court in Charleston. Attorneys Melvin Belli and Monte Preiser asked $5 billion in compensatory damages for victims and $10 billion in punitive damages in connection with the leak. In the week after the accident, Carbide's stock plummeted $11 per share. An OSHA inspection of the Institute plant found it safe.

Six days after the event the Soviet Union entered the debate. Tass reported the Bhopal tragedy was the result of the criminal policy of "profit at all costs" pursued by Western big business.[10]

The same day, Union Carbide scientists were allowed to enter the Bhopal plant, and Anderson met with Indian Foreign Secretary M. K. Rosogotra, "for general discussion of the entire situation."[11] Carbide's executive officer was asked to leave the country quickly because his safety could not be guaranteed. Before he left India, Anderson, in response to questions about the cause of the leak, told NBC News, "Somebody has to say that our safety standards in the United States are identical to India or in Brazil or someplace else, and that what they do here, we've been doing for years. Same equipment, same design, same everything."[12]

The official death toll stood at 1,900.

In Dunbar, West Virginia, the state health director admitted he was concerned about the Institute plant but noted the area's emergency evacuation plan was a "model for the nation."

By December 10, Bhopal authorities declared the city's air and water safe. An Indian scientist in Calcutta asserted the leak had ruined $5.2 million in crops and could leave the land barren for years.

Belli was shown on the network news wearing a dark blue pinstripe suit with a shiny pink handkerchief stuffed in a jacket pocket, and Washington lawyers John Cole and Arthur Louis arrived in India to prepare their suits. The Associated Press noted Belli gave a beggar woman the equivalent of $1.74 and told a reporter she had made a "good haul."[13]

As the jets disgorged American lawyers, India's Central Bureau of Investigation issued a preliminary report stating poor plant safety measures caused the leak. The Bhopal city council announced its intention to bring a multimillion–dollar suit over the incident. Doctors reported new gas exposure cases and said they worried that a possible epidemic of viral pneumonia might sweep the injured.

Back in Danbury, Connecticut, Carbide corporation headquarters, Anderson announced the firm would contribute $1 million to a relief fund. A few days later, the Indian government refused to accept the money.

The following day the corporation released documents from the 1982 Bhopal inspection, noting the serious safety problems at the facility.

Mother Teresa, who urged people to "forgive . . . forgive" arrived in Bhopal December 11, the same day interns and apprentice doctors walked out on strike after a Bhopal city councilman allegedly struck a senior doctor over the release of a gas victim. Rumors spread throughout the city as busses arrived with troops. Schools and colleges were ordered closed until December 20.

That same day in Paris, the French environmental minister asked Union Carbide to ship twelve tons of MIC scheduled for delivery at the Port of Fos elsewhere.

On December 12, the previous day's rumors were proved fact. Union Carbide announced it would neutralize the remaining MIC at the Bhopal plant by processing it into pesticide the following weekend. Residents panicked, and an estimated 200,000 began to flee. Doctors returned to work.

The ripples from the disaster continued to wash ashore in various places in the United States. In testimony before the Asian affairs subcommittee in Washington D.C., Robert Peck, deputy assistant secretary of state for Near Eastern and South Asian affairs, said the United States might have to reconsider its lack of a general policy to encourage or force U.S.-based corporations to follow safety standards set by American law in all operations.

In Chicago, an American relative of six Bhopal victims filed a class-action suit against Union Carbide for $50 billion, and another investor in New York filed suit for $1 billion as compensation for devalued stock.

In response to the escalating legal claims, Connecticut Attorney General Joseph I. Lieberman proposed an out-of-court settlement. "Disaster relief should not come in pinstripe suits," he noted.[14]

On December 13, the MIC turned away by Brazil arrived safely at the Union Carbide plant at Woodbine, Georgia.

On Thursday, December 14, Rep. Stephen Solarz, chairman of the House Foreign Affairs subcommittee on Asia and the Pacific, announced he would fly to India to assess the disaster's impact on U.S.-Indian relations.

Solarz was one of few people entering the city; many residents, the government estimated between 150,000 and 200,000, had fled in preparation for the MIC neutralization, which had been dubbed Operation Faith. Refugee centers were established, primarily for slum residents who lived near the plant. However, they remained largely underpopulated. Three helicopters, equipped with water tanks to defuse any errant gas, were readied for the neutralization process, and paramilitary troops were deployed near the plant. Indian scientists reported no trace of toxic chemical around the plant, and two doctors hired by Union Carbide held a news conference to announce that long–term damage to lungs and eyes as a result of gas exposure might not be as severe as originally feared.

The same day, Rep. Henry Waxman's House subcommittee on health and the environment met in Institute. In what many characterized as surprising testimony, Anderson told the committee his firm was now willing to support increased government regulation of the chemical industry. "Bhopal has changed the world" Anderson said. "It is overwhelming all of us at Carbide."[15]

Dr. Peter Infante, of OSHA, testified the Institute plant emitted 11,000 tons of chemical waste into the atmosphere each year, some of it known cancer-causing agents. He characterized Union Carbide as "one of the good guys" of the chemical industry.

In Chicago, an irate Union Carbide shareholder sued the company's directors and asked that they be held personally responsible for his and other stockholders' losses. No specific dollar amount was requested.

On Sunday, December 16, Operation Faith began. It continued without incident through December 22 when the last of the MIC was neutralized. However, during the conversion process workers discovered there was much more MIC at the Bhopal facility than originally believed, and ultimately about twenty-four tons of the chemical were converted. By the time the process was completed, the city had begun to return to normal.

Because of the extensive aftermath and population displacement—as well as for political reasons—the New Delhi government postponed Bhopal-area voting in the parliamentary elections area until late January.

During Operation Faith, attorney John P. Coale, who said he was representing the city in a lawsuit, said he would seek an out-of-court settlement.

In Europe, a spokesman for the German firm of Bayer Antwerpen NV, which also makes MIC, said an accident like the one in Bhopal was impossible at the Bayer plants. However, the spokesman noted that discussion of more stringent regulation of the chemical industry was under way in the European Economic Community.

The French turned away a chartered Danish freighter from Fos and sent sixty-eight barrels of MIC back to Norfolk, Virginia.

On December 21, the Indian government began to close the Bhopal refugee camps.

The same day the Union Carbide plant in Woodbine, Georgia, laid off sixty workers, but the firm canceled the move several hours later.

And, on December 20, Union Carbide hired the public relations firm of Burson-Marsteller, which handled the Tylenol poisoning scare, to restore its public image.

Reconstruction

During the next few months, the focus of the Bhopal disaster shifted from providing immediate victim relief to reconstruction. Discovering the long-term impact of the disaster became a priority for the Indian government and scientists studying the event. In addition, the issue of "blame" moved center stage, both in the United States, where lawsuit followed lawsuit, and in India which, in addition to court action, began to implement political policies to avoid future disasters.

On the political front, in late December Rajiv Gandhi won an electoral landslide, although Bhopal voters did not go the polls until late January when they, too, cast their votes for the Congress-I Party. However, Bhopal voter turnout was characterized as low owing to calls to boycott the election because of the disaster. On December 28, the labor minister of Madhya Pradesh, the Indian state of which Bhopal is the capital, resigned, taking moral responsibility for the accident. The state government also fired its chief inspector of factories and suspended two other senior officials of the labor ministry.

As part of the long-term policy debate on the issue, Gandhi maintained India would continue with its technological modernization program. In June 1985, speaking to the annual conference of the International Labor Organization, Gandhi said the Bhopal disaster underlined the need for more stringent controls on the activities of multinational corporations in Third World countries, and he urged transnational corporations to abide by a well-defined code of conduct.

The government used other tools. On December 23, officials refused to renew the operating license for the Union Carbide Bhopal plant. The renewal request had been filed about six weeks before the disaster occurred. On July 3, 1985, more than 250 Indian Carbide employees were arrested for demonstrating at the state legislature, protesting the government's failure to provide them with new jobs. The plant closed on July 11.

The government established a special legal aid committee to help Bhopal victims. "We do not want the tragedy to be exploited by foreign lawyers," H. R. Bhardway, minister of state for law, said. "Advocates in India are competent enough to deal with such cases. We will use all channels, even diplomatic, if necessary, to insure that the sufferers are suitably compensated."[16]

One channel for such activity was the Indian parliament which, in April, prohibited American or other non-Indian lawyers from representing Bhopal's victims in the ever-increasing number of suits. American attorneys, not to be denied potential billion–dollar fees in the cases, sued the Indian government.

The government itself also turned to the courts. The attorney general recommended the government sue Union Carbide in American courts, where potential damage awards were generally acknowledged to be much larger than Indian awards. Robins, Zelle, Larson & Kaplan, the Minneapolis law firm which had represented plaintiffs in the Dalkon shield and MGM Grand Hotel fire cases, was appointed, buttressed by a team of Indian attorneys. The government filed formal suit on April 8 in U.S. District Court in Manhattan after rejecting an out-of-court settlement offer of $230 million from Union Carbide. Press reports emphasized the government had characterized the offer as ridiculously low.

Through a series of preliminary reports, which culminated in an official government document released almost a year after the tragedy, the Indian government charged Union Carbide with negligence in the accident. The formal report, portions of which were printed in the *Christian Science Monitor* in late March, alleged there were design flaws, operating errors, defective systems and managerial mistakes contributing to the accident. Union Carbide's Indian subsidiary was held jointly responsible. The report agreed with Carbide assertions that water in the tank was the proximate cause of the leak, but suggested that engineers, in what may have been a cost-cutting measure, might have connected two previously independent sets of pipes leading to a device to neutralize any escaping gas, in violation of initial design specifications.

Events in Bhopal centered on the interwoven issues of determining the scope of the disaster and providing victim relief. In late December, the first in a series of mental health studies of the victims characterized the impact of the disaster as very bad. "People just won't believe anybody anymore. They won't believe the government. They won't believe the doctors, and they won't believe Union Carbide," the report stated.[17] By June 1985, two medical studies found fairly widespread mental problems resulting from the leak, among them neurotic depression, anxiety and neurosis, primarily among women.

On January 1 and 12, and again 100 days after the accident on March 12, hundreds of demonstrators stalled traffic on city streets and railroads demanding financial and medical relief. Some were arrested. The demonstrators lambasted not only Union Carbide but also the state government for failing to inform them of the potential toxic threat posed by the gas.

The physical effects of the leak took longer to document and were more hotly debated. Early in December, D. S. Varadarajan, director-general of the government's Council of Scientific and Industrial Research, said the government had found traces of phosgene and chloroform in Bhopal, a charge Union Carbide chemists denied.

Almost two months after the accident, on January 20, the *Hindustan Times* reported Bhopal residents were continuing to die as a result of the leak. The newspaper said twelve people had died earlier in the month and that doctors had found traces of toxic chemicals in their blood and organs. New complaints, among them a burning sensation in the stomach coupled with diarrhea and loss of appetite, were being reported by patients. Autopsies showed severe gastrointestinal damage, which doctors attributed to the leak. It was not until about two months after the accident that doctors discovered that an antidote for cyanide poisoning also worked well for MIC, despite the enormous differences between the two chemicals.

An investigation by India's top medical research body, results of which were released in late January, found Bhopal's victims suffered "devastating" lung damage and secondary damage to their brains, livers and kidneys. One year after the accident, about 60,000 Bhopal residents were unable to complete a day's work due, in many cases, to impared lung function.

The issue of potential birth defects had been raised at the

outset of discussion of the possible long-term consequences, and on January 24 the *Times of India* reported more than 150 stillbirths and abortions in Bhopal since the leak. In April, Bhopal hospitals reported an increase in the number of premature births and a decline in birth weights in the children of women exposed to the leak. However, doctors could not link these findings directly to the leak itself.

A year after the accident, most scientists and doctors agreed that almost one-fourth of the women in the first trimester of pregnancy at the time of the accident had miscarried, given birth prematurely or borne handicapped children. Other women reported a rash of gynecological problems which Indian doctors and scientists believed were related to the leak.

Elsewhere in India, chemical accidents became major news stories. On January 5, forty-five workers at a textile mill in Koratty, 270 miles southwest of Madras, were hospitalized after a chlorine leak. No one died. Six days later, more than 100 people were treated for eye and throat irritation after nonlethal gas leaked from a warehouse in Jabalpur, 382 miles southeast of New Delhi. Bhopal was not immune. On April 1, a chlorine leak injured seven people and caused widespread panic, and press reports revealed there had been a similar chlorine leak in the city on March 28.

As if to keep pace with events in India, on January 10 in Karloskago, Sweden, a huge cloud of sulfuric acid leaked from the Nobel Chemical plant, resulting in the evacuation of 300 residents and the medical treatment of 200 persons. No one was killed, although it took the cloud about twenty-four hours to dissipate.

The following week, the International Labor Organization, headquartered in Geneva, reported that every three minutes a worker dies on a job-related industry accident. The report emphasized the problem was particularly acute in developing countries. In June a global coalition of 300 environmental, consumer, church, union and farm workers launched a worldwide campaign to end the use of the twelve most hazardous pesticides, many of which had been banned in the United States but were still in use in the developing world. MIC was not among the twelve, although DDT and dioxin were included.

Activity in the United States followed what was becoming a global pattern.

The American Connection

There were two intitial issues in the American Bhopal debate: could it happen here, and can Union Carbide survive?

The first issue was initially addressed by a flurry of news reports focusing on chemical production in the United States and the development of community evacuation plans. One Associated Press story suggested that catastrophe or near catastrophe brought improved safety planning, but that the wisest course was not to wait for such an impetus.

The federal government apparently heeded the advice. On January 11 the Environmental Protection Agency (EPA) announced it could find no major safety violations at the Institute plant. OSHA's report on Institute could be considered only as ironic in view of future events. In early 1986, the agency levied a multimillion–dollar fine against Carbide—the largest in United States history—for safety violations at the plant.

The environmental agency also said it would continue to examine the release of toxic chemicals into the Kanawah River, the primary waterway in the Charleston area. However, the EPA said the releases posed no health hazard. A study of evacuation plans for the Charleston area by the Federal Emergency Management Agency concluded, "Some of the plans, as presently organized, need to be improved to effectively deal with the wide range of hazardous situations that can occur."[18]

However, the text of the EPA study was leaked about a week later, casting doubt on the originally publicized conclusions. New information indicated that, in 1983, about 840 gallons of MIC had been spilled, at various times, in the Institute plant. Actual losses into the environment could not be computed, but the EPA found that the majority of the releases were the result of normal accidents. It characterized the plant's overall compliance with environmental regulations as above average.

A week later, Union Carbide announced the previously reported leaks represented only about one-third of the actual number, but that none of the individual leaks exceeded five gallons.

The corporation said the initial reporting error had been because of the haste with which its report to EPA was prepared. An internal memo released from the EPA on January 24, however, appeared more damning. According to the agency, Union Carbide had known about the possibility of a runaway reaction of MIC at the Institute plant as early as three months before the Bhopal leak. The corporation did not consider the problem an immediate hazard, but rather one that would require correction within sixty days. Administrative remedies, such as more frequent inspections and new training programs, were instituted, despite recommendations from company safety experts that new safety equipment also was needed.

Rep. Waxman, upon learning of the memo, said, "They're warning about the exact same thing that happened in Bhopal. It looks like there's a possibility Bhopal could have been avoided. If nothing was done, I find this a very distressing situation."[19]

The bad news didn't end for the chemical giant. On March 14, it was revealed that the Institute plant had waited four hours before notifying local authorities of a spill in which four persons were hospitalized. Charleston public safety director Ken Carper said he was "totally satisfied" with the company's efforts, but the incident was investigated by OSHA and the EPA.

Two days later, corporate spokesman Jackson Browning said the potential danger of the chemical spill had been exaggerated and that none of the chemicals involved were carcinogenic. But, three days later, federal officials criticized the firm for delays in providing information on plans to resume production of MIC in Institute. And, in Ontario, California, two workers at a Carbide plant were hospitalized and a nearby freeway closed for several hours when a hydrogen gas tank exploded and caught fire as the workers were transferring the gas to a second tank.

"It"—a potentially lethal chemical spill—obviously had happened in the United States. The next day Carbide went on the offensive.

Based on reports from chemists and engineers who had visited the Bhopal plant, the firm announced that the contamination of the storage tank in Bhopal may have been caused by sabotage. Union Carbide of India initially denied the allegation, but about a month later the Indian firm also concluded that sabotage could have been the root of the disaster. Its report, released in India, criticized Bhopal plant workers. According to the parent firm, four months of laboratory experiments had confirmed that between 120 and 240 gallons of water had been introduced to the tank, causing a violent chain reaction. The conclusion was supported by independent experts writing in *Science*.

"The amount of water that got into this tank took a while to get in there. That is why we said it might be deliberate. I can't impugn malice here. I can't say it's an act of sabotage," Anderson said at a news conference.[20]

Yet, a tragedy the magnitude of Bhopal had not occurred in the United States, and political and industry forces set to work to assure themselves, their stockholders and the public that such a tragedy was unlikely now and would become less likely in the future.

In March, the president of the Chemical Manufacturers Association board of directors announced a program to improve emergency response plans. Edwin Holmer insisted the chances of a Bhopal in the United States were slight but, in a significant about-face brought on by what Holmer characterized as a lot of "soul searching," called for greater industry disclosure about dangerous chemicals to state and local governments.

The next day Waxman and Rep. James Floria said they would press for legislation to develop more complete information on toxic chemicals and more stringent regulation of plant emmissions. In a press conference, Waxman charged the chemical industry was dumping staggeringly high amounts of cancer-causing agents and other hazardous materials into the atmosphere. He said a federal failure to regulate would be an abdication of government responsibility. The legislation was introduced in late May, a companion bill to a proposal to expand the EPA's superfund. The proposal also required chemical manufacturers to disclose the toxic substances being produced at various facilities and the development of community emergency response plans.

About a month later, a spokesman for the National Association of Manufacturers attacked the bill as seriously flawed because it did not balance the cost of compliance with the actual risks posed by emissions.

However, the charges and countercharges in the political arena were nothing compared to the brickbats flying in American courts. The first billion-dollar suit over Bhopal had been filed within a week of the leak. By the time a year had elapsed, about 100 suits totaling uncounted billions had been filed in U.S. courts, and there was additional litigation pending in India. American relatives of the Bhopal victims sued. The city itself and the Indian government sued. Stockholders sued Union Carbide—for the incident itself and for the decreasing value of their portfolios. One of the worst slumlords in Los Angeles was investigated for filing a Bhopal suit on behalf of relatives of his tenants.

The American litigation was eventually consolidated in the U.S. District Court in Manhattan before Judge John Keenan who, on April 16, urged Union Carbide to establish an emergency fund of from $5 to $10 million for victim relief, with the provision that such a fund would not be construed as an admission of liability. Carbide complied, at the lower figure, and then found its efforts stymied by the Indian government, which refused to accept the money because it considered the expenditure reporting requirements burdensome.

Keenan also asked the American lawyers to nominate two of their numbers to act as counsel on the consolidated action. The lawyers couldn't agree. Keenan named the legal representation, and the lengthy legal battle was set for the key question: should the case be tried in the United States or in India? More than eighteen months after the tragedy Keenan ruled the suit could—and should—be tried in India.

But Union Carbide was taking its economic lumps elsewhere. For about two months after Bhopal, its stock declined significantly. Standard and Poor's lowered its rating of the Union Carbide debt to the lowest investment grade; Moody's followed about two weeks later citing "fundamental weaknesses" in the firm's day-to-day business operations.

At the end of January, financial analysts said they were disappointed in Carbide's fourth-quarter profits, and earnings were categorized as weaker than expected. First–quarter 1985 income fell 34 percent below the 1984 level.

A decline in first-quarter earnings was hardly a problem by

mid-summer. In late June, GAF corporation began what would be considered a hostile takeover bid. The Carbide board of directors, the individual members themselves the target of suits, were initially reported favorably inclined to GAF, but by November the company had decided to fight the move. The financial wrangling had at least one salutary effect: the take-over push and bullish stock market combined to boost Carbide stock to a new all-time high. The lawsuits over the decrease in the value of shareholders' portfolios became moot.

Institute

The first chemical manufacturers in the Kanawah Valley, nestled between the river from which the valley took its name and the Appalachian Mountains, probably were the Shawnee Indians. They developed the technology to extract salt by boiling brine in a hollowed log.

By the 1980s it appeared the Shawnee had been prophetic in their use of the land. The Kanawah Valley was the site of no less than eleven different chemical manufacturing facilites, and in recession-racked West Virginia the industry was viewed as one of the state's most dependable employers. Still, there were concerns, among them statistics which indicated that lung and other respiratory cancer rates in the area were 21 percent above the national norm.

As in its beginnings, Institute, about ten miles from Charleston, remained a minority community. It was largely black and unincorporated.

"Institute is like Bhopal," Estella Chandler, a black teacher of architecture and spokeswoman for a group called People Concerned about MIC, said. "We're in the Third World."[21]

Institute's connection to Bhopal was tangible—the Institute MIC plant, which had been built in the late 1960s, was similar to the Bhopal facility, although the safety systems at Institute were computerized and somewhat more sophisticated than those in Bhopal. In addition, the Institute plant had not suffered from the economic reverses that characterized operations in Bhopal. Workers from Institute had traveled to Bhopal to help set up the plant and train the Indians who would work there.

Local residents were drawn into the debate about just exactly what had happened in Bhopal. On December 12 a Union Carbide engineer living in Nitro, one of the other Kanawah chemical communities, made national headlines when he refused to rule out the possibility that human error could have caused the leak. The engineer, who had spent a month at Bhopal in 1982, said the Indians running the plant lacked the sort of "what if" emergency training that was more common in the American chemical industry.

On December 14, Waxman's subcommittee met in Institute, and Union Carbide agreed to install a chemical-spill warning system at a center for the handicapped located near the plant, while asserting the plant was safe. It was the first of about $5 million in safety improvements in the community and at the plant the company would make in the coming months.

But there was also controversy. In mid-December, Union Carbide was fined $55,000 for nine environmental violations at its South Charleston Technical Center, a few miles from Institute. The company admitted there had been problems and said it was working to correct them.

Three days after Union Carbide denied there were safety problems at the Institute plant, three residents filed a billion-dollar class action suit—on behalf of 10,000 residents of the area—claiming that Union Carbide had knowingly allowed leaks of MIC at Institute.

On March 28, Union Carbide representatives met with community leaders to discuss plans to restart the MIC production process at Institute. About a month later, in mid-April, Charleston officials premiered an upgraded evacuation plan they said would empty the community within twenty to twenty-five minutes. At the same time, the EPA approved the restart of the Institute facility, stating it would not endanger those living in nearby communities. On April 26, a community organization asked Union Carbide to delay the start up until the Indian government released its Bhopal report and an even more sophisticated evacuation plan was developed. Despite some discussion, Carbide decided to continue with its plans. Despite a twenty-four–hour delay for some minor problems, the company resumed production of MIC at the Institute facility on May 4—without incident.

The calm continued until August 11, when the problems of the Third World came home to Institute. A yellow cloud of choking gas leaked from the plant for ninety minutes—injuring about 150 and requiring that about twenty-four people spend the night in the local hospital. Although some of the aldicarb oxide—the gas Carbide said escaped—was neutralized in the recently improved flare ventilation system, about 20,000 people who lived within a ten-mile radius of the plant were warned to stay indoors and to turn off ventilation systems until the chemical dissipated.

The following day Carbide officials admitted they had delayed warning the surrounding communities of the leak for about twenty minutes because the computerized safety system inside the plant had erroneously predicted the gas cloud would remain within the confines of the plant itself. The company asserted the chemical which had leaked was less toxic than MIC, although independent experts disputed the claim and insisted that, had the leak been more prolonged, some deaths would have resulted.

However, regulations which would have allowed the government to fine Carbide for the delay had not yet taken effect. Charleston Mayor Mike Roark was concerned. "They did not notify anybody other than making an initial call to the county," he said. "And, the information that came from them was sparse to say the least."[22]

At the same time, there were pro-Carbide demonstrations in South Charleston where the firm was the city's single largest and most reliable employer.

The very next day another Carbide spill occurred. This time, 1,000 gallons of malodorous brake fluid—smelly but not toxic—were spilled into the Kanawah River. One woman was treated and released from a local hospital.

Simultaneously, the previously reported toxicity of aldicarb oxide was questioned. Rep. Waxman said internal Carbide documents indicated the product was a Class 4 chemical, the same classification accorded MIC on Carbide's internal toxicity scale.

Carbide temporarily suspended production but rejected Waxman's assertions about aldicarb's toxicity.

The next day, West Virginia's attorney general announced he was considering suing Carbide over the Institute leak. Meanwhile, another valley chemical plant, FMC Corp., reported a brief discharge of chlorine gas which, while it did not leave the plant, resulted in the hospitalization—in the intensive care unit—of one worker.

On August 16, amid reports in the *Los Angeles Times* that the primary chemical involved in the August 11 leak had been methylene chloride, which causes malignant tumors in the livers and lungs of rats, Anderson traveled to Institute and said officials were trying to learn how much of the cancer-causing substance was emitted in the leak.

"One god-sent blessing from these leaks is that now people in Institute know that something like Bhopal could happen to them," Edward Clark, a retired Charleston policeman, said.[23]

Two days later, about 400 people jammed the auditorium at West Virginia State College to protest the two leaks. They demanded tougher right-to-know laws, and some of those who spoke said Bhopal was "on our minds."

The Institute leak precipitated a pattern of legal maneuvers similar to those which occurred after the Bhopal disaster. On August 20, twenty-four local residents filed a $24.2 million suit against Carbide, charging the company with negligence and stating that the newly installed safety system had failed to provide adequate warning. The next day, eight others filed a suit for $64 million on the same grounds.

The same day the first suit was filed, Carbide announced that William D. Ruckelshaus, the former EPA administrator with a reputation for integrity, would conduct an independent investigation of the Institute leak.

Things quieted momentarily, in part because Carbide was beginning the financial and corporate moves it needed to make to stave off the hostile GAF bid. Then, on September 26, the firm announced it would shut down—for an "overall evaluation"—its Silicon II units in South Charleston, which had cost $150 million to construct less than two years before.

Four days later, OSHA announced it planned to fine Carbide

$32,000 in connection with the Institute leak, asserting the firm had disregarded standard procedures when transferring toxic chemicals. The federal agency noted the company had not implemented engineering controls to prevent air contamination and stated emergency respiratory equipment had not been readily available.

In response, Carbide officials asserted safety procedures at Institute were "careful and comprehensive."

The next day—October 3—the government released a private consultant's report stating there have been at least 6,928 chemical accidents in the United States since 1980, killing 135 and injuring 1,500. Most of the accidents, the report stated, occurred at manufacturing plants, while the remainder took place when various chemicals were being transported.

Bhopal, it turned out, was not the only community to suffer from the "normal accidents" associated with the chemical industry.

NOTES

1. This recreation of the events of Bhopal was developed from the various news accounts on which this study is based.

2. Stuart Diamond, "The Bhopal Disaster: How It Happened," *New York Times*, January 28, 1985.

3. Deborah Mesce, "Domestic News," Associated Press, December 10, 1984.

4. "Most at Plant Thought Poison Was Chiefly Skin–Eye Irritant," *New York Times*, January 30, 1985.

5. There is still significant dispute about the death toll in Bhopal. The official Indian goverment estimate remains 2,700 dead; reports at the time of the accident generally cited these higher figures.

6. Peter S. Hawes, "Details of Gas Leak Could Be Weeks Away," Associated Press, December 4, 1984.

7. Harbaksh Singh Nanda, "International News," Associated Press, December 5, 1984.

8. Tina Chou, "Death Toll Rises, Doctors Report Still Births," Associated Press, December 6, 1984.

9. Tina Chou, "International News," Associated Press, December 7, 1984.

10. "Soviet Media Report Allegations of Negligence," Associated Press, December 8, 1984.

11. Tina Chou, "International News," Associated Press, December 8, 1984.

12. Ibid.

13. Victoria Graham, "Belli Says It's a Case of 'Great Union Carbide and the Poor Indian,' " Associated Press, December 10, 1984.

14. "Domestic News," Associated Press, December 12, 1984.

15. Anderson's comment was carried on the Associated Press and all three television networks December 14, 1984.

16. "Gandhi Government Offers Free Legal Aid to Union Carbide Victims," Associated Press, January 3, 1985.

17. Earleen F. Tatro, "Life in Gas-Stricken City Gradually Returns to Normal," Associated Press, December 24, 1984.

18. "Washington News," United Press International, March 15, 1985.

19. David Goeller, "Washington Dateline," Associated Press, January 24, 1985.

20. Dennis C. Milewski, "General News-Carbide," United Press International, March 20, 1985.

21. Daniel Leon, "General News: Chemical Leak," United Press Intrernational, August 19, 1985.

22. Pam Ramsey, "General News: Leak," United Press International, August 12, 1985.

23. "General News: Leak," United Press International, August 16, 1985.

Escaping gas blanketed
much of Bhopal

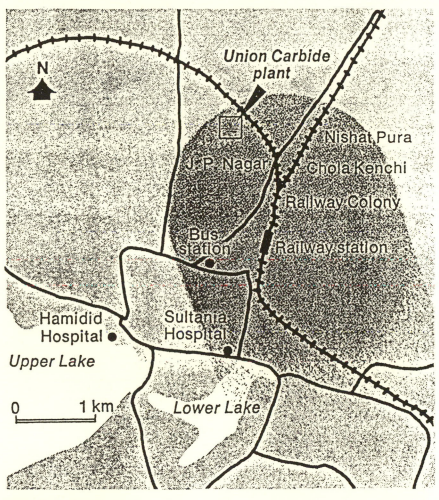

Map of Bhopal.

2
The Scholarly Framework

Perhaps one of the more easily foreseen results of the Bhopal disaster is this study, for Americans found almost all of what they knew about Bhopal from the mass media. This media reliance occurred primarily because Bhopal was an international story—the sort of event few Americans have the chance to witness first hand. And Bhopal was big news. The Associated Press editors ranked it the second most significant story of the year—behind only Ronald Reagan's reelection—and more significant than the widely reported African famine.

Bhopal provided an almost ideal story to study how the mass media would cover such an event and the underlying issues of "normal accidents" and "technological hazards." The issue itself also provided a unique way to study how and why people remember and respond to media coverage of a particular event. What parts of the Bhopal story were memorable to those who saw it on television or read about it in newspapers and magazines? Why might some parts of the story have been more memorable than others? And how might those concerned with understanding the mass media as well as understanding the entire issue of technological hazards use such information to make more certain that the next chemical leak results in fewer deaths and injuries and more public understanding?

These are a few of the questions this study makes an attempt—although only an initial one—to address. As is usual with such enterprises, the way has been paved by some insightful scholars who suggest, if nothing else, some preliminary paths to explore.

THE MEDIA MILIEU

Technological hazards, and the mass media, are modern inventions. Their interaction, therefore, has been the subject of little pointed research. However, recent mass communication scholarship has focused on two more generalized areas that may have some bearing on the media's coverage of technological hazards: media reportage of science, and coverage of environmental issues, some of which are considered technological hazards. Thus, theorizing about media coverage of technological hazards must combine work from three distinct scholarly areas: research on the role of the mass media in the reportage of hazards, media coverage of science and media reportage of environmental issues.

A general conclusion emerging from research on the behavioral aspect of hazard management is that the mass media can play an important role in public learning about the nature and possible consequences of natural hazards (Sorenson, 1983; Saarinen, 1982; Ledingham and Masel-Walters, 1985). These roles are described by the National Research Council's Committee on Disasters and the Mass Media as: (1) preparing the public to meet emergencies; (2) providing mitigation, warning and coping information; (3) providing reassurance and a mode for grieving or assuaging guilt in the aftermath of a tragedy; (4) providing mobilizing information; (5) assessing the postdisaster period and the lessons that have been learned; and (6) providing a record of activities related to the natural hazard.

Recent studies indicate the public finds the mass media among the most useful sources of information about a variety of natural hazards (Sorensen, 1983; Wenger, 1980), although media reportage is often augmented by a reliance on personal experience and discussion with significant others in a decision to evacuate (Ledingham and Masel-Walters, 1985). The media can serve to set the community agenda in areas of political debate (McCombs and Shaw, 1972), including the area of environmental issues (Atwater et al., 1985), and 49 percent of the American public indicate an interest in science-policy issues, among them hazards issues, covered in the mass media (Cronholm and Sandall, 1981). Specific media campaigns on single issues, asbestos awareness (Friemuth et al., 1981), and environmental problems, for example, energy conservation (Winert et al., 1984), have been found effective. Thus, on one level, a

> "powerful effects" model is emerging, wherein mass communication is seen to have the potential for exerting strong influence on audiences. Mendelsohn and Maccoby and Farquhar show that if mass media campaigns are prepared carefully according to communication theory principles, present messages repeatedly over a period of time, target messages to specific audiences and tie the message themes to a clearly specified campaign objective, then there is a good chance the campaign will have important effects on attitudes and behavior (Sood, 1982:10).

Such a conclusion assumes a purposeful use of the media. Yet the very nature of news coupled with the demands of newsgathering and production may lead the media to distort reports in certain specific ways. "However, the message of theory seems to be that we might better regard media content as a unique cultural form, a 'media culture' fashioned according to its own conventions and forming a more or less independent element in the social reality rather than a message about that social security. Thus, even where media act as carriers for other institutions, they tend to alter substance, to conform to the demands of 'media culture.' " (McQuail, 1983:219).

One well–documented element of this media culture is the "coups and earthquakes" syndrome in the reporting of Third World events. Developing nations have complained, with ample scholarly support (Bledsoe, 1982; Gerbner, 1961; Gerbner and Marvanyi, 1977; Larson, 1979; Lent, 1977; Mujahid, 1970; John Robinson, 1967; Weaver, 1981; and Wilhoit, 1983), that "1,000 bodies in the developing world equals equals 100 bodies in Western Europe equals one body in an American community." Such reportage is a marked contrast to the changes in gatekeeping roles in local reports of natural disaster outlined by Waxman (1973).

Mass media coverage of Third World events tends to focus

on issues of large–scale disaster—either natural or technological—and on well-developed lines of political and social conflict.
While such a stance obviously has much to recommend it for
coverage of technological hazards such as the Bhopal disaster,
its more subtle influence may mean that certain elements—for
example, drama and political conflict—may monopolize media
reportage while the more scientific and politically complex questions raised by the event may be ignored as the impact of thousands of dead and injured wanes. One study (Drabeck and
Quarantelli, 1967) found such a pattern in local coverage of domestic disaster, and similar trends in domestic news coverage
of environmental issues have been found (Hungerford and Lemert, 1973). For example, during the gasoline crunch of the early
1970s, the media reacted to the environmental problems rather
than serving as a predictor of the event (Dangerheld, McCartney
and Starcher, 1975).

A second major element in the "media culture" is the my-
thologizing elements of news—particularly television news.
Scholars have noted a "structural difference" between television
news and news conveyed by the print media, which has generally been categorized as a reliance on storytelling, drama and
conflict on the part of television. Other scholars, however, have
noted that myth is a process of developing cultural meaning
(Knight and Dean, 1982), with increased amounts of imagery
which may reinforce existing images in society (Hofstetter, Zukin and Buss, 1978). At least one student of the ultimate technological hazard, nuclear war, has said that television and film
provide a means of imagining the unimaginable (Lifton and Falk,
1982); but the quality and content of that image have been the
subject of no formal study.

Finally, the accurate transmission of messages via the media—
as filtered through the media culture—has been the subject of
some study. Many American communities place contact with
the media in a somewhat secondary role in disaster planning
(Clark, Carter and Leik, 1979). Specifically, the accuracy and
quantity of media warning messages vary directly with media
contact—and the forthrightness of that contact—with crucial
government agencies (Sorensen, 1982). While scholars give the

media generally high marks for the reportage of the "large facts" of natural hazards (McKay, 1984), errors in the coverage of smaller details, such as crowd estimates, have been found a significant portion of the time (Scanlon, 1978). In addition, newspaper coverage of natural disasters tends to include many stories for which no source is cited, while radio stations tend to withhold information based on the perception that the public could be easily panicked in a natural disaster (Kueneman and Wright, 1975).

These somewhat positive findings in the area of media accuracy are generally offset when the issue shifts to technological hazards. Media reportage of the Three Mile Island incident did not fit "reality" in several areas (Stephens and Edison, 1980, 1982; Krieghbaum, 1979). Reporters from the nation's "best" media outlets, for example, the *New York Times*, lacked the necessary scientific expertise to ask the proper questions about the technical events of Three Mile Island (Stephens and Edison, 1980, 1982). The result was that reporters "missed" certain key facts which then allowed them to paint a more reassuring portrait of what was happening at the plant than was actually the case. Media economics—that is, the need for the media to make a profit by reaching a large audience and thus shading coverage away from the extremes of scientific debate—also has been blamed for withholding certain sorts of programs from the public (Keller, 1979).

While scholars have noted that the media made "large" errors in the coverage of Three Mile Island, reporters and editors were not without some help. The utility company, early during the incident, established a policy of volunteering nothing, answering only those specific questions which were asked. Other scholars, for example, Trost (1984), have noted a similar trend in the chemical industry. Finally, on a more generalized note, the media have been found reluctant to contact—and in many instances unable to understand—scientists discussing these often technical and frequently controversial issues (Mazur, 1981; Cronholm and Sandall, 1981). The result has led some scholars to conclude, "On scientific issues with political overtones, such as nuclear power, fluoridation, etc., dialogue seems essential. The public's fantasies, thoughts and questions may not be most effectively answered by the mass media" (Cronholm and Sandall:94).

Thus it would appear that scholarly research on the media's role in hazard awareness seems to point in two opposing directions. On the one hand, hazards researchers insist that the media can be one of the most effective means for public education about scientific questions, among them hazards. Such a use of the media involves rather complete journalistic access to and use of messages designed to inform the public. On the other hand, analysis of actual media messages about hazards indicates that some of the information the public needs to receive is never made available to the media or that reporters and editors lack the education and training to understand information they do receive. In addition, some scholarship would indicate the media tend to distort messages in certain predictable ways, based on the conventions of the newsgathering process. It is apparent that some broad understanding of both the quality and content of messages printed and broadcast by the media about a technological "accident" such as Bhopal may provide richer and more complete understanding of the media's role in public education about hazards. Critical events theory provides a crucial matrix by which to analyze—both quantitatively and qualitatively—media messages about technological hazards.

CRITICAL EVENTS THEORY

Critical events theory seeks to explain how the media report significant events. Studies in this area of media scholarship are message centered, and "seek to identify those events which will produce the most useful explanation and predictions of social change" (Kraus, Davis, Lang and Lang, 1975:99).

Because critical events theory is message centered, it assumes media messages are more than mere bits of information relayed to the public.

A significant message (that is, one that has broad impact) may portray an event in a strikingly dramatic way. Such messages should not be regarded as merely sensational or pandering to popular taste. Rather, they may serve to put events into a context that facilitates public understanding and use (that is, they present communication events in human terms) (Kraus et al., 1975).

Technological hazards such as the Bhopal disaster are, by their very nature, the sort of events that lend themselves to a dramatic media retelling. As Tuchman (1973) has noted, such a routinization of the unexpected in the newsroom tends to emphasize what happened—rather than why—conflict— rather than analysis—and hard news—that is, event-oriented coverage—rather than predictive reportage. Some scholars have labeled such a clustering of emphases distortion. However, Tuchman has argued:

> distortion itself is a socially constructed concept. The construction of reality through redefinition, reconsideration and reaccounting is an ongoing process. The newsmen's typifications indicate that it might be valuable to think of news not as distorting, but rather as reconstituting of the everyday world (Tuchman, 1973:129).

Critical events theory suggests research into four separate areas: the thematic content of media messages; the interplay between communicators and their sources; public attention to and use of messages; and the credibility—or public acceptance— of the messages.

Content analysis can address two of these issues: the thematic content of media messages and, at least to some extent, the interplay between communicators and their sources. Further, considering past scholarship in the area of hazards research, media coverage of hazards and media coverage of science, critical events theory would suggest several research questions. They are:

- To what extent do media reports emphasize the issues of hazard mitigation and preparedness? Does media coverage focus on the event itself rather than these underlying issues?
- Does media reportage of the specific event parallel the five stages of a disaster as understood by hazards scholars?
- Do journalists emphasize some sources, for example, public officials,

and spend little time with others, for example, the average citizen or doctors and scientists? Are events emphasized rather than issues or individuals?

• Does the media's tendency to emphasize drama and conflict also include an emphasis on individual helplessness?
• Does the pattern of television coverage follow that of print reports?

In addition, a more qualitative investigation of the thematic content of media reportage of the Bhopal disaster may illuminate the underlying process of providing social symbols to help create meaning. The mass media's contribution to this collective funded memory of the event may, in turn, have important implications for media coverage of other hazards and for public discussion of the issue.

METHOD

Because Bhopal was an international event, few individual newspapers and television stations sent reporters to the scene. Instead, as with almost all major international stories, the bulk of the coverage which reached the American public was provided by the three commercial television networks, the wire services, the East Coast "prestige press," several of which also provide "wire service" coverage to newspapers throughout the country, and the national news magazines. Scholarly research also has indicated that most international events drop quickly from the news agenda. Bhopal proved an exception to this rule, in part because Union Carbide was an American firm, in part because the month of December is traditionally a "slow news" month and thus there was more space for international coverage, and in part because the separate events which comprise the "Bhopal tragedy" took several weeks to unfold. Indeed, as of this writing, a number of crucial issues about the disaster have yet to be resolved.

Because of the unique nature of the event itself, the content analysis was conducted for a two-month period, beginning December 3, 1984, with the first report of the tragedy, and continuing through February 3, 1985. February 3 was selected as the cutoff date because, while news from Bhopal had not ended, it had diminished significantly and the major events of the disaster had been completed. Further, many studies of media coverage have focused on only a week or two of reports—a time frame hazards scholars would argue ignores much of the recovery period and any long-term analysis of the event.

Since most Americans now indicate they get most of their news about the world around them from television, news reports broadcast on all three commercial networks—including the video coverage—were included in the study, a total of thirteen stories from ABC, fifteen from NBC, and thirteen from CBS. For those Americans who obtained their news from the print media, the wire services provided the great majority of international news coverage. Thus, all reports carried on the Associated Press (N = 214), United Press International (N = 132) and Reuters (N = 177), the major British news service, were acquired. Until the past year, a study of only AP and UPI probably would have been sufficient; however, with UPI's recent financial woes and the expansion of Reuters into the American market, Reuters became important for the analysis. Two representatives of the prestige press, the *New York Times* (N = 166) and the *Washington Post* (N = 57), both of which sent individual reporters to Bhopal, were included in the study, as were three major American newsmagazines: *U.S. News and World Report* (N = 8), *Time* (N = 27) and *Newsweek* (N = 10).

Television news coverage of the event was acquired from the Vanderbilt University Television Archives, which records the nightly news from all three networks as it is broadcast on the East Coast. The Vanderbilt archives are the scholarly standard for the study of television news coverage. Print material was acquired from the Nexus data base, which carries all that is printed in more than sixty different media outlets in the United States. Nexus is updated daily and is available in libraries. Many large news organizations also use Nexus to augment their own libraries. The data base was searched for any story which related to Bhopal, or to Union Carbide or to Institute, West Virginia, during the study period. A single mention of any of the key words—Bhopal, Union Carbide or Institute—called up the story from the data base. Thus, stories which mentioned Bhopal, but which were not focused exclusively on the event, were included in the study. Articles printed in the *Times of India* were obtained through a hand search of the publication.

The data-base search produced about 1,500 separate articles. However, because all three wire services run morning, evening and broadcast "cycles"—which may include duplicate stories— wire service reportage was culled to eliminate those duplicates. If a story was only slightly modified between cycles, both versions of the story were analyzed. The *Washington Post* and *New York Times* coverage also was culled for stories which were purely wire reports and labeled as such. In addition, the *New York Times* coverage was culled to delete the daily news summary, since the summarized articles would be analyzed separately, and the weekly "news quiz," in which Bhopal was a correct response for several weeks of the study. In all, 952 stories were analyzed.

A coding schema for print reportage and transcripts of the television coverage was developed. Those items coded included: story source; dateline; general story subject; the three most frequently cited sources in the story; type of story—for example, editorial or letter to the editor, investigative report, analysis or coverage of separate events; the primary thematic focus of the story—Bhopal, Institute or technological hazards; the inclusion of social or cultural background in the story; the inclusion of information about long-term health, environmental, legal or economic impacts in the story; and the phase of the disaster into which the story fit. The most powerful figure, the person or institution portrayed as capable of influencing the outcome of events, also was coded for each story.

Finally, all stories were ranked along a helplessness scale, ranging from extreme—that is, an item in which a central figure is presented in such a way as to suggest a complete inability to have affected the outcome, good or bad, which accrued—to mild—that is, an item in which a central figure is presented as having had a good chance of affecting outcomes but for some reason is unable to do so. Central figures in the helplessness analysis included institutions as well as individuals, and there also was a "not relevant" segment of the scale for those items having no bearing on response-outcome dependence or independence or items in which the central figure was represented as having caused desired outcomes. Seven coders trained for three weeks on the coding instrument and achieved an overall degree of intercoder reliability of 80 percent—although reliability among coders on many items was much higher.[1] An intercoder reliability level of 65 percent on instruments which require some judgment and analysis is considered acceptable. A separate instrument for the coding of the visual material in the television stories was developed and tested. Intercoder reliability on the visual analysis was 95 percent.

THE PUBLIC RESPONSE

Messages do not end with the media. People receive them, remember them and sometimes act on them. An analysis of the public response to media messages is the second leg of critical events theory, and scholarly research in that area also suggests some paths to follow. For example, Mileti et al. (1975) report that newspaper circulation increases during the immediate post-disaster period, but tends to decline during the reconstruction phase of the event. This may indicate the media know viewers and readers well, and hence provide the kind of coverage which will most attract them, or that readers and viewers, finding information suitable only to one aspect of a particular event, turn away from media reports when they no longer meet individual needs.

There is also a significant body of research which deals with public response to warning information. While most of this scholarship considers the media as only a conduit rather than as an active participant in the warning process, several findings are important to the study of the possible effects of media coverage.

Families warned about impending hazards in one way seek to confirm that information through other sources (Mileti et al., 1975; Ledingham and Masel-Walters, 1985). Such a behavior pattern includes warnings issued through the mass media, although the number of warnings received is inversely related to the attempt to seek additional verification. Journalists' fears of panicking an audience (Kueneman and Wright, 1975) with warning messages may be unfounded. Studies indicate that panic is a highly individualized response and that "most people confronting disasters do not become wildly disorganized and irrational" (Mileti et al., 1975:78). Mileti's work also reveals that newspapers display a rapidly rising interest in disasters, but that newspaper coverage declines once the dramatic aspects of the situation are replaced by replanning and rebuilding.

Such scholarship does little more than point in any one theoretical direction, but it suggests, however tangentially, that readers and viewers may come to the mass media for hazard information for somewhat specific uses and gratifications. These various expectations could lead to different patterns of media use among various groups and to other consequences, some of which might be unintended—depending on the message received. Under this model, the audience is assumed to be active and goal directed. While research based on the uses and gratifications approach has focused on many media uses, of particular import is the consistent finding that the media are used by the public as a means of enviromental surveillance.

> In the information field, for example, the surveillance function may be traced to a desire for security or the satisfactions of curiosity and the exploration drive; seeking reinforcement if one's attitudes and values may derive from a need for reassurance that one is right; and attempts to correlate informational elements may stem from a more basic need to develop one's cognitive mastery of the environment (Katz, Blumler and Gurevitch, 1974:24).

Psychologist Abraham Maslow focused on this last point in his study of human motivation. Maslow postulated that, in a hierarchy of human needs, security is second only to fulfillment of certain physical needs (relief from hunger or pain) in the order of human motivation. Maslow's need hierarchy, in order of importance, is: (1) physical needs; (2) security or predictability; (3) affectional (belongingness and love); (4) dignity (self-esteem); and (5) self-actualization (Maslow, 1954). Maslow noted that in psychologically healthy adults, the need for security "is seen as an active and dominant mobilizer of the organism's resources only in real emergencies, e.g. war, disease, natural catastrophes, crime waves . . . " (Maslow, 1954:42). Thus, reportage of technological hazards could easily fulfill the psychological need for

security. Considering these basic psychological needs and be-
haviors, some of which already have been well documented in
both communications and hazard research, the type of reportage
of natural hazards provided by the media may have immense
impact, particularly if the viewer or reader perceives the message
as psychologically salient on any of a number of levels. As
McGuire has noted:

> At first glance it might seem that mass communications offer
> little gratification for the kind of humanistic need stressed by these
> autonomy theories. The daily fare of our newspapers and tele-
> vision programs seems not to offer much help toward becoming
> an integrated, autonomous personality, secure in the knowledge
> that one is captain of one's fate and master of one's soul. How-
> ever, it may be that the average member of the public has some-
> what more modest identity aspirations. . . . The factual material
> of the media provides integrating themes and an opportunity to
> identify, in fact or at least in fantasy, with movements that tran-
> scend one's own gratification for one's autonomy and integration
> needs (McGuire, 1974:179).

If media messages about natural hazards do speak to such
fundamental psychological needs, then it is particularly important to correlate specific message content with the use made of
it.

THE HUMAN USES OF DISASTER REPORTAGE

The foregoing would suggest that the mass media, in its reportage of technological hazards, could fill an individual need
for environmental surveillance. People might read or watch
more news—and retain more about what they have seen—if that
information is perceived as salient to the task of environmental
awareness.

In addition, retention of facts and images from stories about
a technological hazard also may be influenced by individual
feelings of "helplessness or powerfulness" with respect to similar technological hazards or to past experiences with either technological hazards or natural hazards, such as tornadoes,
earthquakes, floods, and so on.

Finally, individual perceptions of the event itself may also be "colored" by general media use patterns. Previous scholarship would suggest, for example, that heavy television viewers would retain fewer "facts" about the event, while heavy print consumers would be more able to answer factual questions (see, for example, Patterson, 1980). However, much of this scholarship has focused on the possession of facts to the exclusion of memory of visual images—a type of media use which may be particularly important in disaster-like settings where imagining the unimaginable may be important to understanding and responding to a particular event.

METHOD

Two 400-person telephone surveys were conducted during the first weeks of July 1985, about seven months after the gas leak in Bhopal occurred. The metropolitan Charleston, West Virginia, area, the site of the sister Bhopal plant and of ten additional chemical plants, was the locus of one survey while Eugene, Oregon, a community which is 150 miles from the nearest technological hazard—the Trojan nuclear power plant—functioned as a control. The two communities, according to the 1980 census, are similar in population, education and income levels, percentage of white-collar as compared to blue-collar residents and, at the time of the interviews, unemployment rates. Standard survey procedures for random number generation were used, and respondents were assured of the confidentiality of their surveys. The author monitored a number of the individual interviews—which were conducted by a professional polling firm—to insure interviewer understanding of the survey and the manner in which questions were asked. On several key questions in which respondents could have fallen into a specific response pattern, the interviewers alternated where they began in the series to minimize the possibility of patterned response. A total of 395 interviews were completed in the Eugene area, 394 were completed in the Charleston area. Response rates were within "normal" range for "number-plus-one" random digit dialing process.

So much for framework. The initial issue, then, is to outline what the media said and showed about Bhopal.

NOTE

1. Reliability levels were assessed according to a procedure reported by W. A. Scott, "Reliability of Content Analysis: The Case of Nominal Scale Coding," *Public Opinion Quarterly*, 19:321–325, 1955.

3

Bhopal in Black and White

THE MEDIATED OVERVIEW

Any mass mediated reality is a composite comprised of what the media said, reflected and enhanced by individual perceptions. Walter Lippmann in his early work in public opinion perhaps phrased it best:

> The only feeling that anyone can have about an event he does not experience is the feeling aroused by his mental image of that event.... In all these instances we must note particularly one common factor. It is the insertion between man and his environment of a pseudo-environment.... I mean a representation of the environment which is in lesser or greater degree made by man himself (Lippmann, 1949:9–10).

The events of Bhopal were, to paraphrase Lippmann on two different levels, both made and represented by man. While the issue of the potentials and dangers created by technological hazard are not the subject of this study, the media's representation of those potentials and dangers most certainly is. And that mediated representation is, in some fundamental ways, a pseudo-reality of the sort of which Lippmann spoke.

That reality—the composite of all media reports—could be characterized as coverage of a dramatic event, focusing on the crisis of the moment while leaving longer-term issues of impact and mitigation distinctly in the background. There were fine distinctions within the composite, just as there are fine distinctions of color and shade in any portrait, mediated or not. But the overall picture provides evidence of the mediated reality of which the theorists speak—a pseudo-reality which may have important consequences for not only those who cover the news but also those who must, in various ways, respond to it.

Emphasis on the Event

Most of the stories—74.8 percent—were published or broadcast during December, timing which reflects the media's general emphasis on the dramatic event rather than long-range implications. Almost all the newsmagazine coverage fell in this period. The most notable exception was the lengthy investigative series on the events leading up to the leak which was published in the *New York Times* about seven weeks after the event occurred. The *Times* was the only publication included in the study to attempt this sort of extensive investigation, and the results of the *Times*'s work were generally not disseminated in the other media outlets.

This emphasis on the event itself rather than the policy issues raised about the event was evident in a number of other ways. About 85.1 percent of all the stories focused on discrete events within the larger Bhopal crisis: events in Bhopal itself (23.3 percent); Union Carbide and the Indian government's response (25.0 percent); and similar events in other countries (6.0 percent). The overwhelming emphasis on the components of the event itself also meant that the generalized issue of technological hazards received little coverage: 10.5 percent of the stories had, as their primary focus, technological hazards and an additional 8 percent used the issue as a secondary focus.

This lack of generalization from the specific to the conceptual is particularly noteworthy because 21.6 percent of the stories printed or broadcast had as a primary or secondary focus events in Institute or in the United States. For example, an Associated Press series on the potential for similar accidents in the Golden Triangle of Texas, published in December, examined only Texas rather than using problems in the Golden Triangle to highlight and describe similar problems throughout the United States.

While such a focus might have overburdened a single story or even an in-depth series, none of the media outlets studied chose to do "follow up" work in other areas of the country or the world. The event-oriented nature of the coverage was reflected in one final way. Of all the stories printed or broadcast about the event, 62.6 percent contained little or no discussion of any long-term health, environmental, legal or social impact of the disaster. Of those stories which did mention long-term consequences, about 30 percent included discussion of health issues while 25 percent focused on the legal questions—primarily Union Carbide's potential liability in the case and the travels of American lawyers to India in search of potential clients.

Preparedness Is Not an Issue

The event-oriented coverage leads naturally, in some sense, to the second major constellation of "media coverage traits": a lack of stories in the predictive and warning phases of the event. About 34.6 percent of all the stories studied fell into the impact and postimpact response phases of the disaster. An additional 47.8 percent focused on long-term rehabilitation and reconstruction. While 12 percent of the stories were impossible to categorize as to "phase of the disaster," that left only 5.6 percent of what was written and broadcast about Bhopal as preparedness or warning.

The deeper issues of the Indian views of the "whys" of the Bhopal tragedy received even less attention. Only two stories, one in Reuters and the other in UPI, mentioned the Green Revolution or the fact that India has been able to feed itself for most of the past ten years. Only 2.6 percent of the stories discussed, in any detail at all, the economic and political reasons the plant was built in India. None of these stories included any sort of institutional analysis of the issue, although letters to the editor in *Time* and the *Manchester Guardian* employed it.

Different mediums, of course, provided slightly different emphases. Thus, within the larger media composite, certain important variations did emerge.

THE WIRES

Most Americans who read newspapers get their foreign news from the three wire services: Associated Press, United Press International and Reuters. Most large metropolitan dailies subscribe to all three services, and many of their reports blend reports from the three wires. However, the majority of small newspapers rely on United Press International, the least expensive of the three services. The Associated Press, as does UPI, provides reports not only for the print media but also runs a special broadcast wire that is used by many television stations. The three networks also heavily supplement their own foreign news coverage with reports from the Associated Press and United Press International broadcast wires. Thus, much of what Americans were told about Bhopal, to some extent regardless of medium, came to them filtered through wire service reports. While wire service coverage followed the same pattern as the generalized portrait the media presented, there were significant differences in how the three services covered the story.

Covering the Basics

Because the wires sell themselves, in part, as the various bureaus that comprise them, it was expected the wire services would carry reports about Bhopal—and the implications of the disaster—from a number of places. Yet there were significant differences (Chi square = .0001) in the datelines of the various wire service reports. Reuters tended to concentrate its coverage on the events in India. Thus, while 43 percent of all the wire service reports originated in Bhopal, New Delhi or other Indian communities, Reuters datelined 53.8 percent of its reports from the subcontinent. Associated Press filed 40 percent of its Bhopal reports from India itself and UPI followed closely, filing 38.4 percent of its stories from the subcontinent.

Reuters also stuck closely to traditional news sites in the United States, for, after India, it filed its largest segment of reports from Washington, D.C. and New York—18.9 percent. On the other hand, the Associated Press and United Press International—perhaps because the two services are more closely linked to individual newspapers in less–traditional news centers, filed the second largest segment of their reports from Danbury, Connecticut, Carbide corporate headquarters, and Institute, West Virginia, the home of the sister Bhopal plant. AP filed a total of 25.7 percent of its reports from those two places and only 11.7 percent of its reports from New York and Washington, D.C. UPI filed 21.5 percent of its reports from Danbury and Institute and only 10.7 percent of its reports from New York and Washington. Reuters, on the other hand, filed only 9.8 percent of its reports from Danbury and Institute. This significant divergence in dateline foreshadowed many of the other differences among the wires: The American wire services connected Bhopal much more closely to certain sorts of events in this country than did British-owned Reuters.

Story subject matter reflected another set of distinctions, these perhaps more based on the relative economic health of AP and Reuters when compared to UPI (Chi square = .009). Associated Press presented, in terms of general subject matter, the most in-depth coverage of the three wire services. Of the AP reports, 19.3 percent concerned events in Bhopal or India itself; fully 50.8 percent of the reports focused on the Indian government's, the American government's or Union Carbide's response to the events; 19.9 percent of the reports covered various issues and events relating to technological hazards; and 9.4 percent of the stories concerned the economic ramifications of the leak. Reuters followed a similar pattern—23 percent of its reports centered on events in Bhopal or India, while the response of the two governments involved and of Union Carbide was the subject of 37.2 percent of Reuters reports. The generalized issue of hazards was the subject of 16.5 percent of Reuters coverage, and 19.8 percent of what the wire service ran focused on the economic ramifications of the event.

UPI, on the other hand, focused almost all of its coverage on events in India and the responses to them. About 32.5 percent of UPI's reports concerned events in India and 40.1 percent of its stories reflected various responses to those events. However, only 15.3 percent of UPI's stories concerned hazards and only 10.8 percent focused on the economic ripples.

In this sense, UPI's coverage was more event–oriented; the

other two wire services connected the leak to other places significantly more often, although AP did a better job of broadening the story than did Reuters.

The event orientation also was reflected in the type of stories the wire services filed. While 88 percent of all wire stories covered discrete events, 91 percent of UPI's coverage and 90.0 percent of Reuters's reports were strictly event–oriented. Associated Press, on the other hand, devoted 85 percent of its coverage to events and 12.6 percent of its reports to issue analysis. AP was the only wire service to file any investigative or analysis pieces.

However, all three wire services spaced their coverage equally throughout the study period, reflecting the wires' ability and willingness to provide coverage of continuing developments within the larger story that was Bhopal. This continuity of coverage was not present in magazine reportage of the event or in television's coverage. While Bhopal was often mentioned in the lead paragraph of wire reports, a little more than one-fourth (27.8 percent) of the wire stories did not mention Bhopal until lower in the copy, thus indicating the leak had become a "news peg" for other sorts of stories. Finally, the wires told their readers the geographic location of Bhopal in about 21.2 percent of all the stories carried—a form of orientation that was not as common in the other media studied, although television and magazines compensated with maps. The differences among the three wires on geographic orientation did not quite reach accepted levels of statistical significance (Chi square = .0578), but both Reuters and AP provided a geographic location for Bhopal in about 24 percent of their stories. UPI, on the other hand, provided such information in only 15.3 percent of its reports.

The Focus on Technological Hazard

The issue of technological hazards—and how the wire services covered it as it became part of the Bhopal story—amplified the previously noted patterns.

While 40.5 percent of all wire reports had as a primary focus events in Bhopal itself, Reuters was even more Bhopal-centered than were the other two wire services. Thus, 54.5 percent of the

Reuters' stories had a primary focus on events in Bhopal while an additional 29.5 percent of the Reuters' pieces used events in Bhopal as a secondary focus. Bhopal itself was mentioned tangentially in 15.9 percent of the Reuters' reports.

Reuters also provided the most extensive coverage of events in Australia, primarily threats against Union Carbide, something the other wires reported only briefly. The historic link between Great Britain and its Commonwealth partner may have contributed to the attention Reuters focused on the area.

While the Reuters focus was international, AP and UPI expanded their coverage more to related American stories. Only 30.8 percent of the AP stories had Bhopal as their primary focus while events in Bhopal were a secondary focus of an additional 35.5 percent of AP's work. Thirty-three percent of AP's stories mentioned Bhopal only tangentially. UPI's coverage reflected the same emphasis, although not to the same degree. Of the UPI reports, 41.8 percent had as their primary focus events in Bhopal while 34.5 percent reflected a secondary focus on events there. Twenty-three percent of the UPI stories mentioned events in Bhopal in only a cursory fashion (Chi square = .0007).

Thus the two American wire services Americanized what would, at least at first glance, seem to be an Indian story. Reuters, perhaps because of Great Britain's historic ties to India, or perhaps because it was relatively new to the American market, played the story from a much more strictly Indian point of view.

While two of the wire services Americanized the story, they did not Americanize the events in Bhopal by linking them directly to West Virginia. Only 8.9 percent of AP's coverage had as a primary focus events in Institute and only 7.5 percent of its reports gave secondary emphasis to those events. Almost three-fourths, 74.8 percent, of AP's reports did not mention Institute or its connection to Bhopal. UPI followed suit. Only 8.5 percent of its reports focused primarily on Institute, and additionally 10.7 percent had Institute as a secondary story focus. Institute was not mentioned in 72.8 percent of UPI's coverage.

Reuters provided only the most tangential of links between Bhopal and Institute. Institute was the primary focus of 6.8 percent of the Reuters reports, the secondary focus of an additional 2.3 percent of the wire reports. Fully 85.6 percent of the Reuters accounts did not mention Institute and its connections to the events in Bhopal. There was no statistically significant distinction between the three wire services in this respect, despite the minor percentage fluctuations.

Although the wires expanded the Bhopal story to include events in the United States, coverage was generally not expanded to include discussion of the larger issue of technological hazards. Only 5.5 percent of all the wire service reports used as their primary focus the technological hazard issue: 5.6 percent on AP, 6.8 percent on UPI and 3.8 percent on Reuters. A secondary focus on technological hazards was a little more frequent—it occurred in 6.9 percent of all reports: 5.1 percent in AP, 10.2 percent in UPI and 5.3 percent in Reuters. The issue was mentioned tangentially even more often, in 10.7 percent of the stories run on AP, 6.2 percent of those run on UPI and 5.3 percent of the work on Reuters. However, more than 78 percent of all the wire service stories written about Bhopal did not mention the issue of technological hazard—78 percent of those carried on AP, 76.8 percent of those run on UPI and 81.1 percent of those delivered by Reuters. Only 2.9 percent of the wire services' reports, with no statistically significant difference among them, attempted to define the concept of technological hazard.

Clearly, the more conceptual issue of technological hazards was low on the wire service list of what was important about the Bhopal event. However, the two American wire services did, in at least a minority of their reports, attempt to draw the reader's attention to the existence of a similar problem in the United States and other industrialized countries.

The Long-Term Issues and Background

Such an emphasis on events in India and in the United States pushed reports of long-term issues and the background that would have made them more understandable to the reading public low in wire service reports.

The victims of the Bhopal disaster were portrayed as one lump of hurting humanity—"the 2,000 dead and 200,000 injured"—in 88.3 percent of all wire coverage. People could be identified as individual victims with individual stories to tell in only 55 of the 511 wire service reports.

This tendency to lump the victims together in the form of those who were dead and those who were injured manifested itself in other ways. Seventy-seven percent of the wire service stories about Bhopal did not discuss the long-term health and environmental issues that the Bhopal disaster raised.

Yet the wire services diverged significantly in how they treated the long-term issues (Chi square = .0132). The AP mentioned long-term health issues in 16.1 percent of its stories; Reuters mentioned the health issues in 18.5 percent of what it ran. Environmental questions were discussed in 10.7 percent of the AP reports and 9.7 percent of the Reuters stories. However, UPI provided almost no coverage of these same questions, mentioning health issues in only 1.8 percent of its stories and environmental concerns in only 2.9 percent of its reports. Clearly, those media outlets that had access only to UPI were able to provide their readers with significantly less information about the long-term issues than could those newspapers, television and radio stations which had access to the other two wire services.

Another of the long-term issues raised by events in Bhopal was just exactly who—or what—was to blame for the accident. The canons of objectivity—not to mention the litigious nature of the event itself—made this a particularly difficult issue for the wires to tackle. Generally, wire service reports did not cite any person, any piece of equipment or any institution as "at fault" in the accident. More than 78 percent of the stories included no such indication. However, in 13.8 percent of the reports, Union Carbide was blamed for the leak, generally in quoted statements by attorneys who had become involved in the issue. The Indian or American governments were blamed in an additional 3.3 percent of the stories. Longer-term questions—for example, the role of technology in general or the demands of Third World food production—were almost never cited as contributing to the accident in wire service reports, although Reuters in one story discussed the demand the Green Revolution had created for agricultural technology such as pesticides.

The short-term, event-oriented view was reflected in other ways. Cultural information, particularly cultural background on

India and Bhopal, was almost totally absent from wire service accounts. Of those stories in which such background would have been appropriate, only 2.7 percent, or 14 individual stories, included such information. The cultural information most frequently discussed was the presence of slums near the Bhopal Union Carbide plant and the difference in Hindu and Moslem burial practices.

Economic background was treated in a similar fashion. More than 87 percent of the wire stories in which it would have been appropriate included no such information. The economic reasons the plant was built in India—or the possible ramifications of the leak in India—were included in only 2.5 percent (thirteen) of the wire service accounts.

However, while the wires did not provide much in the way of cultural and economic background, and while they did not use events in Bhopal as an entree to discussion of the larger issue of technological hazard, they did broaden the story in another way. Discussion of the accident's economic impact on Union Carbide's corporate health, in the United States or in India, was included in 10.3 percent of the wire accounts. Thus the wires Americanized the economic questions surrounding Bhopal, but linked them with only one issue: would Union Carbide survive. Discussion of the underlying economic factors was never really made available to readers—at least those who relied on the wire service accounts.

Such a wire service portrait of Bhopal is unsettling for those concerned with predicting hazards and lessening their impact. At least on the level of prediction, the wire services failed. Only 2.7 percent of the wire accounts focused on any warning or prediction that an event such as Bhopal might occur. However, almost half the wire service reports—48.9 percent—included discussion of long-term hazard preparedness and mitigation issues. Often these reports centered on the outcome of lawsuits or the economic woes of Union Carbide, but there were many stories which discussed possible additional government regulation of various industries, the costs and progress of rebuilding, community awareness and other issues which are rightly considered a part of the mitigation process. Moreover, considering the impact of billion-dollar lawsuits, the ultimate outcome of court cases should not be excluded as having a potentially important—if very long–term—mitigating influence.

While more than one-third of the wire coverage was exclusively event-oriented, readers who were exposed to wire reports could have learned some important facts about hazard mitigation and become aware of some of the questions the mitigation process raises. The wire services differed significantly (Chi square = 4.00) from each other in this respect. Of all the AP stories, more than half fell into the long–term rehabilitation and reconstruction phase of the event—57.9 percent. Of the stories UPI ran, 42.9 percent dealt with the reconstruction phase, and Reuters played the story amost exactly the same way with 42.4 percent of its reports to reconstruction.

The foregoing analysis, of course, deals with what was made available to editors. Those editors—often referred to as gate-keepers in the scholarly literature of journalism and mass communication—selected only a small portion of the wire service reports to print in newspapers or to broadcast on radio and television. This study does not focus on what decisions the thousands of editors throughout the United States made when deciding what—and what not—to use of the Bhopal story. But the indications that certain sorts of facts—and certain sorts of stories—were hardly ever available for editors to choose makes an even more central point about the role of the media culture. Bhopal, by the time it reached the United States through the wire service reports, had become a story of an event, with some connections to this country. However, those connections were generally short-term and superficial. Long-term issues—of health, the environment and economics aside from corporate survival—were seldom explored, while the more combative and dramatic contests in the courts, in Congress and in various regulatory agencies moved center stage. Individual involvement—even as a victim—was absent, and the issue of culpability was clouded. Attempts at prediction were nonexistent, and the issues of mitigation were separated from the cultural and economic facts which might have given them more substance.

Bhopal had become connected to the worldwide problems of technological hazard in a curious way. The media culture as expressed through wire service accounts made preventing an-

other event, rather than the conditions that gave rise to it, par-
amount. And, as a mitigation strategy, such an approach has
been marginally successful at best.

THE PRESTIGE PRESS

Eastern elite newspapers have, at least for scholarly purposes,
been grouped under the label of the "prestige press." Lately,
that label has also found its way to the *Los Angeles Times*. While
the United States has no official paper of national record, those
publications generally considered members of the elite newspaper core function in that role. For the purpose of this study,
it was important to determine, first, how the prestige press—in
this instance the *New York Times* and the *Washington Post*—covered the story, and second, if that coverage differed from the
wire service and magazine approach. Such an analysis is one
way of gauging whether different information about Bhopal
reached national decision and policy makers, who generally read
the elite publications, as opposed to the larger public, which is
the biggest consumer of wire service reports.

Covering the Basics

Like the wire services, both prestige publications studied sent
their own reporters to India to cover the Bhopal story. In addition, the *New York Times* hired several Indian journalists, who
worked for other national periodicals, to augment its on-the-
scene reporting staff. Both newspapers used relatively few
"pure" wire reports in their Bhopal coverage. What each paper
ran was produced, in large part, by its own reporters, who may
have supplemented their own information with wire service material but who did much of their own independent reporting.

However, both newspapers did not write the same story. The
New York Times, consistent with its image as newspaper of national record, produced what was the most comprehensive reporting on Bhopal done by any of the American outlets studied.
The *Times*, for example, was the only news organization to do
any significant investigation into the event itself—and much of
what the paper published in late January was confirmed months

later by investigators in both India and the United States. The *Times* also provided more purely scientific insight into the story than did any other outlet. It was the first, for example, to run an article devoted exclusively to the chemical and toxic properties of MIC—and that article appeared less than forty-eight hours after the accident itself. An AP story with similar details was filed soon after. The *Times* provided its readers with some in-depth cultural background about India and Bhopal. *New York Times* readers learned, for example, that the local Hindu dialect included a word for MIC which, when translated into English, meant "medicine for crops." Given this linguistic connection, and the well–understood need for continued food production on the subcontinent, the act of those Bhopal residents who ran toward the plant—and into the gas—becomes more understandable. Such elements did not statistically pervade the *Times* coverage, but they were included in the reports, and they did provide a portrait of Bhopal which was unique in its depth and breadth.

The *Washington Post*, on the other hand, recounted a different version of the Bhopal story. The newspaper of the nation's capital reported on the politics of Bhopal. Bhopal stories found their way into congressional hearing rooms and into the federal agencies the *Post* covers as part of its regular reporting on the national political community. The *Washington Post* did not separate Bhopal from the political reaction to the event—and thus treated its readers to yet another view of the tragedy.

These generalizations, however, provide but the skeleton for the reportage. The mediated reality of the prestige press was, in many ways, similar to other reports in other outlets. The emphasis changed, but the overall story remained very much the same.

The Particulars of the Event

Perhaps because the *Times* considers itself a paper of national record, its coverage of Bhopal was—in terms of the number of stories printed—much greater than that provided by the *Post*. A total of 166 stories which, in some manner, concerned the Bhopal issue appeared in the *New York Times*. During the study period only fifty-seven such stories appeared in the *Washington Post*. The greater numbers, however, did not necessarily lead to other distinctions.

Both papers published the bulk of their Bhopal stories during December, 74 percent in the *Times* and 64.9 percent in the *Post*. There was little distinction in the type of story published, with the exception of investigative pieces. The *Times* ran ten such stories, 6.9 percent of its total coverage, while the *Post* ran none. However, the bulk of the reports in both newspapers focused on the discrete events that made up the larger Bhopal story. About 61 percent of the coverage in both publications was event–oriented; 27.1 percent of the *Times*'s stories focused on the various issues comprising Bhopal while 36.7 percent of the *Post*'s stories reflected an issue focus. If the investigative pieces the *Times* ran—which included reports on the larger issues of Bhopal in addition to investigation of specific events—were included in the issue-story total, then the percentage of issue coverage in both publications during the study period was almost identical.

However, the datelines of the stories in the two papers reflected each publication's different conceptual emphasis. About 38 percent of the *Times*'s stories carried a Bhopal or India dateline compared to 22 percent of the *Post*'s stories. However, 17.5 percent of the *Post*'s reports were datelined Washington D.C. or the Charleston, West Virginia, area; the *Times* datelined only 12.0 percent of its reports from those places. One anomaly in the reports was that almost half the *Post*'s reports—49 percent— did not carry a specific dateline. Only 21.1 percent of the *Times*'s reports fell into this category. The general newspaper practice is not to dateline stories from the "home town." While the papers did not always follow this policy, stories without a specific dateline generally did arise from either New York or Washington D.C., respectively. If these stories were added to the specifically datelined stories, then the difference in emphasis between the publications becomes even more pronounced.

The somewhat broader coverage of events by the *Times* also was reflected by international datelines on 12.7 percent of its reports while those datelines were found on only 5.3 percent of the *Post*'s stories (Chi square = .0003).

The second statistical indication that the two papers told somewhat different stories about Bhopal was subject matter of the various reports. The response to the event, including government response, clearly reflected the distinction. More than two-fifths, 42.0 percent, of the *Post*'s reports had, as a general subject, response to the event. For example, the *Post* ran an excellent article on the issue of risk-benefit analysis which focused, to a major extent, on the issue of societal risk. While there were many ways to report on such an issue, the *Post* chose a political frame, quoting then-EPA director Ruckelshaus saying, "We must assume that life now takes place in a mine field of risks from hundreds, perhaps thousands, of substances. No more can we tell the public, 'You are home free with an adequate margin of safety.' "[1] In contrast, the subject of response to the event was the focal point of only 20.8 percent of the *Times*'s stories.

Events in Bhopal itself were the focus of 28.9 percent of reports in the *Times*, but only 20.0 percent of those in the *Post*.

The *Post* also covered the economic angles somewhat differently—24.0 percent of its stories were on the generalized subject of the economic impact of the event while only 20.1 percent of the *Times*'s stories fit that category.

Thus, at least in terms of subject matter, the *Post* chose to tell its readers about Bhopal in terms of governmental and economic response to a specific event. The *Times*, while it reflected this emphasis, placed a much greater emphasis on the "story behind the story"—the role of technological hazards in modern society. Bhopal made an arresting news peg for such reporting, but the *Post* did not take advantage of it as the *Times* did.

While there was some distinction between the papers in the emphasis given to coverage of the event itself, the two news organizations differed more often in the way they chose to relate the events of Bhopal to other questions, either events in Institute, concerns about Union Carbide or the more abstract issue of the impact and mitigation of technological hazard.

In 35.5 percent of the *Times*'s stories and 35.1 percent of the *Post*'s work, Bhopal itself was the primary story focus, and events there became a secondary focus in an additional 33.1 percent of the *Times*'s reports and 40.4 percent of the *Post*'s stories. Bhopal was mentioned tangentially in 30.17 percent of the stories in the *Times* and 24.5 percent of the *Post*'s reports.

The percentage differences were not statistically significant. However, the *Times* provided its readers with a specific geographic location for Bhopal significantly more often than did the *Washington Post*. About 24.1 percent of the *Times*'s stories carried the specific reference while only 8.8 percent of the *Post*'s stories did so (Chi square = .0217).

Yet, when the focus shifted to West Virginia, important distinctions emerged (Chi square = .0001). Institute, and events there, was a primary focus in only 5.4 percent of reports in the *Times* while it was the major focus of 7 percent of the *Post* stories. However, Insititute played a prominent secondary role in the *Post*'s coverage—it was the secondary focus in 22.8 percent of the publication's reports while the *Times* made it a secondary focus in only 3.0 percent of its reports. Institute was mentioned tangentially in 17.5 percent of the *Post*'s reports but in only 5.4 percent of the *Times*'s coverage. Thus, the *Post*'s readers had far more opportunity to become aware of the Bhopal–Institute connection than did *New York Times* readers.

Institute, of course, is geographically much closer to Washington than it is to New York, which could have accounted for some of the difference. In addition, congressional subcommittees and various agencies like OSHA and the EPA made extensive trips to Institute during the study period. The *Post*, as part of its regular coverage of national government, would have been more likely to cover such activities. The *Post*'s Institute coverage also included two excellent profiles of the community, the second of which also included reports on the problems of transporting hazardous wastes in the Kanawah Valley.

However, it is important to note that, even in the *Washington Post*, Institute and its relationship to Bhopal were mentioned only 52.6 percent of the time. In the *Times*, 86.1 percent of what was printed about Bhopal never mentioned Institute or its connections to the events in India.

The *Post*'s localization of the story—perhaps because it had so many political and regulatory overtones—was apparent in yet another way. About 17.5 percent of the *Post*'s reports had, as their primary focus, the generalized issue of technological hazards; 10.2 percent of the *Time*'s stories included such a focus. In addition, 10.5 percent of the *Post*'s stories used hazards as a secondary focus while only 5.4 percent of the *Times*'s reports did so. And hazards were mentioned—at least tangentially—in 17.5 percent of the *Post*'s reports but only 10.2 percent of what the *Times* printed.

Thus almost three-fourths, 74.1 percent of the *Times*'s reports, included no mention of the issue of technological hazard while almost half, 45.6 percent of the *Post*'s stories, did so (Chi square = .0510). Despite these apparent differences, neither publication thought the term itself was worth formal definition. Only 3.5 percent of the *Post*'s stories and 6.6 percent of the *Times*'s reports carried any definition of the concept itself.

The foregoing would seem to indicate that the *Washington Post*, in many ways, provided a more "in depth" portrait of the questions surrounding the Bhopal leak than did the *New York Times*. However, when specific information contained in the stories was analyzed a different view emerged. The *Times*, to a statistically significant degree (Chi square = .0304), included more information about the long-term health and environmental problems stemming from the leak than did the *Post*. Almost one-third, 29.5 percent, of the *Times*'s stories contained some discussion of the long–and short-term medical and environmental problems the leak had created. Only 13.5 percent of the *Post*'s stories carried such information. Almost one-fifth, 19.5 percent, of the *Times*'s stories also included some information about the long-term legal and regulatory impact of the event; 15.4 percent of the *Post*'s stories included such coverage. Thus discussion of various questions of long-term impact—at least health and environmental issues and, to a lesser extent, legal questions—was included in almost half the *Times*'s stories, 48.7 percent. By contrast, almost three–fourths, 71.2 percent, of the *Post*'s stories did not include such discussion.

This attempt to bring some contextual depth to the discussion was reflected in yet another distinction between the two publications. While the differences were not statistically significant, 7.8 percent of the *Times*'s stories included background information on why the Carbide plant had been built in Bhopal, some background on Indian economic history and some discussion of the impact the Bhopal leak would have on the economic health of the Third World. Such information was included in only 3.5

percent of the *Post*'s stories, although most of those stories centered on the impact the leak would have on Union Carbide's corporate health. However, most of the stories printed in either publication did not consider the underlying economics appropriate, even as background material. About 71.7 percent of the *Times*'s stories and 86.0 percent of the *Post*'s work did not mention it.

Other differences in the contextual depth provided by each paper also may have arisen not from reporting methods so much as the different aspects of the story each paper chose to play. To a statistically significant degree (Chi square = .0001), the *New York Times* provided its readers with far more cultural background than did the *Washington Post*. In those stories where such information would have been appropriate, the *Times* provided it 36.1 percent of the time while the *Post* included such information only 7.0 percent of the time. Of course, there were a number of articles—for example, reports on the Swedish gas leak or coverage of American hearings—where such information would not have been pertinent. However, both papers, even when Bhopal was a focus of the story, generally seemed to assume their American readers would know what it was reporters and editors were talking about without large amounts of background information.

Standards of journalistic objectivity were apparent in several ways, and the two publications did not differ in a statistical sense in how they treated these issues. For example, the bulk of reports in both publications, despite the investigative stories, did not ascribe any blame for the leak. In the *Times*, 68.1 percent of the stories failed to include any comment, quotation or conclusion which laid blame, and an additional 10.2 percent of the reports specifically said no person or entity had yet been blamed for the leak. The *Post* played the issue in a similar fashion. About 73.7 percent of its stories included no mention of blame and an additional 1.8 percent of the stories said no one had yet been blamed for the accident. In those stories where blame was attributed, most often through quotation of lawyers, Union Carbide was the most frequently cited agent. About 9.6 percent of the *Times*'s stories and 15.8 percent of the *Post*'s reports contained quotations or other statements ascribing blame for the Bhopal leak to Union Carbide.

However, because coverage by the *Times* was generally more contextually complex, it treated the entire issue of blame in a more sophisticated manner than did the *Post*. *Times* stories which addressed the issue generally tended to ascribe multiple sorts of blame rather than pointing the accusatory journalistic finger only at Union Carbide or a worker in the plant. *New York Times* readers learned about industrial conditions in the Third World which might have led to the leak. In its investigative series, the *Times* documented the generally deteriorating plant conditions and the poor worker morale. Blame, as reported in the *New York Times*, was often systemic rather than personal.

The two papers also remained objective, or at least impersonal, about Bhopal's victims. An average of 87.3 percent of the reports in both publications did not identify victims as individuals but rather referred to them in the mass. Both newspapers treated the issue of individual victimization in the same fashion, at least in the statistical sense. Only 12.1 percent of the *Times*'s stories and 9.1 of those in the *Post* made it possible for readers to identify individuals who had suffered.

Finally, there was no statistically significant difference in how the two papers covered the event. Prediction was not the order of the day. Only 15.8 percent of the *Times*'s reports and 7.8 percent of the *Post*'s stories could have been considered predictive of the Bhopal leak or similar events, and only 6.1 percent of the *Times*'s stories and 13.7 percent of the *Post*'s reports could have been considered "warning" messages. In contrast, both publications devoted themselves to reporting the event—14.0 percent in the *Times* and 23.5 percent in the *Post*—and covering the rehabilitation and long-term clean up phase—64.0 percent in the *Times* and 54.9 percent in the *Post*. The concept that such industrial events, which have been called "normal accidents" and which are predictable in the sense that in an industrial culture they are likely to occur and reoccur, did not permeate the reportage of even these sophisticated publications. Instead, the focus became what had happened and what was done to clean up the mess.

BHOPAL—ONCE A WEEK

While Americans could read and view reports about Bhopal through wire service coverage published in daily newspapers and on network television reports, newsmagazines had the time to focus in some depth on the story. Magazine readers are, in general, better educated and more deeply involved in particular subjects than are newspaper readers and television viewers. Few Americans get all of their news coverage from the three major weekly newsmagazines; instead magazines are used as a supplement, providing depth of coverage on particular issues. Bhopal was no exception. The story made the cover of *Time* and *Newsweek* on the same day, and *U.S. News & World Report* devoted a significant amount of space—although not the cover—to the event the same week. The similarities ran deeper. In fact, there were few statistically significant differences in the coverage provided by the three publications.

However, there were more subtle shifts.

U.S.News reported Bhopal as an economics story. The details, particularly the details of scientific and medical problems arising from the leak, were but a minor focus compared to the magazine's emphasis on the impact Bhopal would have on Union Carbide's corporate health. *U.S. News* told the story from the economic viewpoint, including a lengthy interview with Anderson as part of its coverage and by noting the legal battle "will spill into other firms making chemical toxics or waste,"[2] in its December 24, 1984 issue.

Time and *Newsweek*, on the other hand, covered the story much more from an event-centered view. Both magazines published vivid descriptions of the actual events in Bhopal and spent a significant amount of space discussing the medical and environmental problems that might arise from the leak. While the economic impact on Union Carbide and the looming legal battles were outlined in both publications, they were reported less prominently. In their place, *Time* and *Newsweek* chose to focus on the more generalized issue of technological hazard and the particular links Bhopal shared with Institute. And, of the two, it was *Time*, particularly in its letters to the editor and in signed essays, which attempted to place the Bhopal event in the context of worldwide technological hazard.

Readers of *Time* and *Newsweek*, and in a different context *U.S. News*, could have begun to make connections between their own lives—and the dangers in those lives—and the events of Bhopal. Magazine coverage, at least in this more subtle sense, played the story as a part of a global drama, still event-oriented but, more than other mediums, connecting that event to some of the lingering questions it raised.

The Specifics of Coverage

All three magazines devoted a significant amount of space to the story. During the two-month study period, *Time* published twenty-seven stories related to Bhopal, *Newsweek* ten and *U.S. News* eight. The difference in story number reflected, to a large extent, the large number of letters to the editor *Time* published. In fact, the type of story published was one of the few statistically significant differences among the three magazines unearthed in the content analysis (Chi square = .0093). *Time* published sixteen "opinion" stories (59.6 percent of its total story count), either letters to the editor or signed columns, while *Newsweek* and *U.S. News* each published only one.

The letters to the editor published also spread *Time*'s reports of the issue over a longer period. All *U.S. News* Bhopal coverage fell in the month of December, and 75 percent of what *Newsweek* published also was printed that month. In contrast, *Time* carried thirteen separate stories in December (48.1 percent of its coverage) and fourteen stories (51.9 percent of its coverage) in January (Chi square = .0109).

With opinion pieces excluded, the three magazines published an almost identical number of stories—eleven for *Time*, ten in *Newsweek* and eight in *U.S. News*. The *U.S. News* stories tended to be somewhat shorter—the magazine published only one piece that ran longer than 1,800 words, and four of its reports were between 825 and 900 words. In contrast, *Time* ran three stories of more than 2,500 words, two stories in the 1,100-word range and three stories of about 1,000 words. *Newsweek* ran one 3,200-word piece and one other 1,000-word story.

All three magazines devoted the bulk of their reportage to issue coverage—*Time* and *Newsweek* each ran six issue-related stories (although the issues discussed reflected the previously noted distinctions) while *U.S. News* ran five such pieces, more than 62 percent of its total coverage.

Subject matter again reflected the subtle differences in coverage. *U.S. News* spread the subject of its reports almost evenly—two stories devoted to the events in Bhopal itself and one story focused, respectively, on the responsibility for the leak, the issue of technological hazard and the general economic thrust of the event. *Time* balanced its coverage with more of an emphasis on hazards, devoting three stories to events in Bhopal, two to the larger issues of legal and corporate responsibility, seven to the generalized issue of technological hazard and nine to the economic ramifications of the event. However, almost all of the pointedly economic discussion of the Bhopal disaster was found in the magazine's letters section. *Newsweek*, too, reflected a similar emphasis. It printed only one story on the economics of the event but three stories on the generalized issue of technological hazards and an identical number on the events in Bhopal itself.

Despite the subtle differences in subject matter, the three magazines provided their readers with much of the same sort of information. Most of the magazine pieces—regardless of publication—did not provide readers with a precise definition of technological hazard (86.7 percent). Two of *Time*'s pieces, however, devoted significant space to discussion of the issue—the only articles in any of the three publications which did so.

Time's broadening of the story was apparent in other ways. Technological hazards were the focus of ten of the publication's pieces—several of them letters to the editor and one an opinion column. The issue was a secondary focus in two other pieces and was briefly mentioned in four more. In contrast, 70 percent of *Newsweek*'s coverage did not mention the issue. And, while 50 percent of the *U.S. News* reports also included either a primary or secondary focus on the question, it was always with an economic—as oppposed to an environmental or health—slant. *Times*'s coverage included all three areas, although the magazine emphasized health and environment more than corporate economic issues.

Despite the secondary emphasis on technological hazards, all three publications gave the events of Bhopal a preponderance of emphasis. While only one story in *U.S. News* used Bhopal as a primary focus (12.5 percent), five other stories (62.5 percent) placed a secondary emphasis on the events in India. Fully 50 percent of *Newsweek*'s coverage focused primarily on Bhopal itself (five stories) and an additional 20 percent (two stories) used events in India as a secondary emphasis. *Time* followed the trend: 66 percent of the stories it printed (seventeen) gave a primary or secondary emphasis to the events of Bhopal.

The Institute connection thus received little emphasis in the magazine reports. The ties to that community were the primary focus of not one *Newsweek* report, and the two other magazines made it the primary focus of only one story. Sixty percent of what was printed in *U.S. News* and *Newsweek* never mentioned Institute; the number of letters to the editor about Bhopal itself meant that 88.9 percent of *Time*'s reports did not mention Institute or Bhopal's connection to it.

Yet the fundamental emphasis on Bhopal itself had a particular point of view. The Bhopal stories focused on political and legal conflict. Most stories contained little information about the economic background to the event. Cultural and social conditions which may have contributed to the accident were discussed rarely; there was no explanation of cultural conditions in India in fully 80 percent of the stories. In those stories which did mention cultural conditions, many focused on details such as the slums around the plant and the various burial practices of Hindus and Moslems. Deeper discussion—for example, of the impact of the Green Revolution—simply was not to be found.

In a similar way, the victims themselves became a mass when photographs were excluded from the analysis. While all magazines published photos of the victims, the printed word tended to lump all the victims together in one hurting group. Fully 81.8 percent of the magazine stories did not paint victim portraits in such a way as to make them distinct individuals. A few stories, four in *Time*, one in *Newsweek*, and two in *U.S. News*, did paint such word pictures. But they were the exceptions, and the photographs published in the three magazines left readers with a vivid visual image that remained largely unmodified or clarified by whatever detail words themselves might have added.

Finally, this general focus on the event, including the minority of stories which did report on the larger issue of hazards, was reflected in lack of discussion of the various long-term questions the accident raised. Only 32.5 percent of the stories included mention—much less extensive discussion—of the possible long-term health and environmental impact of the leak. An additional 17 percent of the stories included some discussion of the long-term legal and regulatory issues Bhopal raised, although none of those stories appeared in *Newsweek*, while 37.5 percent (three stories) of *U.S. News* articles included them, again providing evidence of the magazine's particular slant. Thus an average of 50 percent of the magazine reports—37.5 percent in *U.S. News*, 70 percent in *Newsweek* and 45.5 percent in *Time*—did not include reports about these long-term questions. Only 46.7 percent of the stories could be considered to focus on the long-term rehabilitation and reconstruction phase of the event, primarily the discussion of Operation Faith, and all other reports (exclusive of letters to the editor) were devoted to coverage of the event itself and its immediate aftermath.

Thus, while the magazines did attempt to make some connections between events in Bhopal and larger issues—either corporate stability or technological hazard—those connections were far from systematic. Technological hazards were discussed, but without the sort of information on long-term health and environment, or legal and regulatory questions, which would have rounded out the picture. Economics was the focus of some coverage, but it was traditional capitalist economics stripped of multinational background and connections. What magazine readers got were pieces of the Bhopal picture, event-centered but placed within a somewhat haphazard, larger frame. The frame, however, included some vivid imagery which provided a tone the other print media studied generally avoided.

The Words Themselves

Words, like pictures, have overtones, and on that score the three magazines were very different. *Newsweek* provided perhaps the most sympathetic coverage of the event, from the victims' view. In its cover report, the magazine lambasted the lawyers descending on Bhopal and portrayed the Indian medical effort as somewhat bumbling, collapsing not only from overwork but also from a lack of knowledge. Indian officials were characterized as "mostly slow and self interested."[3] The magazine's reports linked Bhopal not only to Institute but also to the larger issues of transportation of hazardous waste, lack of regulation and the conflict aroused by an industry which brings some jobs to the United States while exporting other work overseas and, in the process, escaping more stringent U.S. industry regulations.

U.S. News provided some potent images for its readers. Its word portraits of Bhopal were among the most vivid and detailed, and it carried the metaphor for disaster from one story to another by describing small children "playing in the shadow of smokestacks" in Institute.[4] *U.S. News* readers were told that the spill had made all of Bhopal, in the words of a witness, "like a big gas chamber,"[5] and a similar image was reinforced in discussion of the chemical "fallout"[6] in the Kanawah Valley and the higher-than-national-norm cancer rates in the region.

Time, because it devoted more space to the event, provided more details. For example, the magazine devoted a small article to a scientific description of MIC and its possible effects. The magazine also coupled compelling pictures with equally compelling word portraits—descriptions of violent coughing spasms and graphic images of dogs eating animal corpses in the days after the disaster.

The magazine provided some of the only background available on Indian history and the history of Union Carbide. *Time*'s readers were told, for example, that Carbide had been essential in the Manhattan Project, the World War II effort first to split the atom and then to develop a weapon based on the result. The nuclear imagery did not end there, for *Time* quoted witnesses to the leak saying they believed Bhopal had been hit by an atomic bomb. In a story focusing entirely on the issue of technological hazard, the magazine and its writers and editors linked Bhopal to hazardous nuclear waste dumping, environmental poisoning with a variety of substances and the Love Canal. Yet, in an effort to balance the story, the writer also noted that "high risk should not be interpreted as imminent danger."[7] Another *Time* story, which outlined the safety record of the American chemical industry, included clearly explained statistics noting that, with exceptions, the industry is considered safe.

Taken as a whole, the magazine portrait of Bhopal was much like that provided by the wire services and the prestige press, if allowances were made for documentable differences in audiences. The publications did provide more depth on some issues, although the larger and more difficult scientific questions were ignored or finessed with quotes from experts but with little effort to place events in context. Still, some connections were possible, and the magazines, to their credit, made a great many of them. Their failure was the failure of most journalism—an emphasis on the immediate and an unwillingness to deal with the long term and complex, although the editors and writers themselves, based on the images and examples they used, apparently recognized that these questions were among the most compelling and newsworthy of the event.

NOTES

1. Cass Peterson, "Risk Benefit Analysis Is Key Tool in U.S. Regulations of Chemicals; EPA Is Divided Over Accuracy of Technique," *Washington Post*, January 3, 1985.

2. Ted Guest with Kenneth R. Sheets and Ronald Taylor, "As Lawyers Move In on India's Tragedy," *U.S. News and World Report*, December 24, 1984, p. 26.

3. Mark Whitaker, "It Was Like Breathing Fire . . . ," *Newsweek*, December 17, 1984, p. 26.

4. William L. Chaze, "Grim Cloud of Worry Reaches U.S." *U.S. News and World Report*, December 17, 1984, p. 16.

5. John S. Lang, "India's Tragedy—A Warning Heard Around the World," *U.S. News and World Report*, December 17, 1984, p. 13.

6. Chaze, *U.S. News*, December 17, 1984, p. 16.

7. Natalie Angier, "Hazards of a Toxic Wasteland; Learning to Cope with High-tech Risks," *Time*, December 17, 1984, pp. 26–30.

This Associated Press photo taken in Bhopal on December 5 was reprinted widely in newspapers in the United States. The caption supplied with the picture indicated that more than 1,000 had died in the leak. Relatives and friends are carrying a body of one of the victims to the cremation grounds. (Wide World Photos)

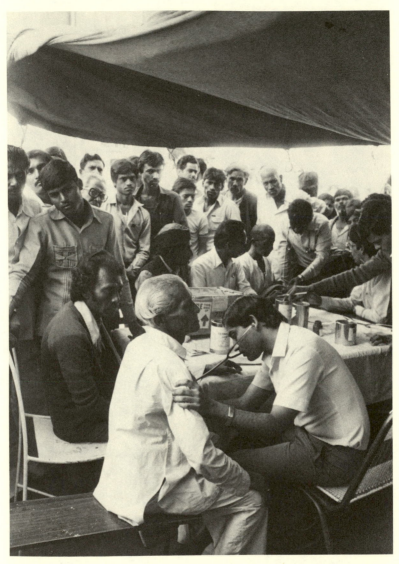

Doctors struck in Bhopal about ten days after the leak. However, they continued to treat patients outside the hospitals. This Associated Press photo is noteworthy because it was one of few mentions of the Bhopal medical effort, and because Indians are portrayed as powerful rather than as victims. (Wide World Photos)

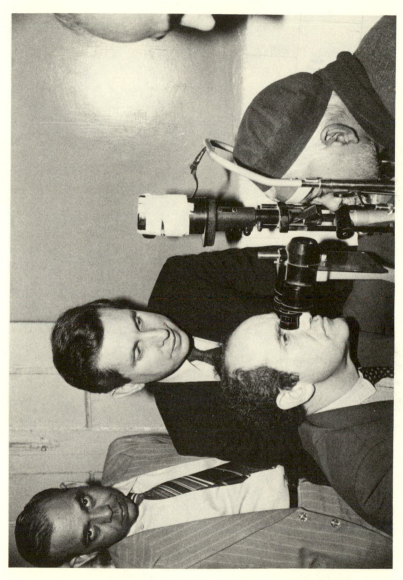

As Congressman Stephen Solarz watches, Dr. Ross Brechner examines the eyes of one of the victims of the leak. Note how Americans are portrayed as active while Indians remain either passive or act as victims. (Wide World Photos)

Photos such as this one of residents fleeing Bhopal after Operation
Faith was announced were widely reprinted in the United States, as
was television footage of the exodus. (Wide World Photos)

The poor of Bhopal fled to government-provided shelters during Operation Faith. Note how women and children receive prominent play as victims of the event. (Wide World Photos)

This Associated Press photo of the Institute plant was widely printed after the August leak in Institute. Television reporters also used the plant as background for standups in many of their reports. (Wide World Photos)

This photo of the Institute plant was taken about six weeks after the Bhopal disaster when the plant was processing MIC that had been returned to the United States from abroad. The caption provided with the photo did not emphasize the similarities—or differences—between what was happening in Institute and what had happened in Bhopal. (Wide World Photos)

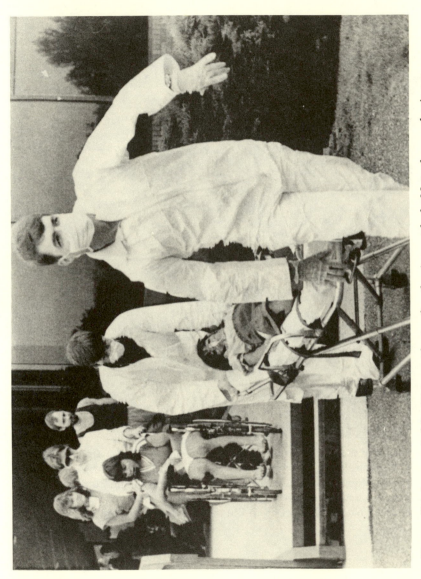

Paramedics transported Institute residents after the August leak. Note the emphasis on women victims in the foreground. (Wide World Photos)

The short-term vs long-term trade-offs individuals are willing to—and sometimes must—make were emphasized in this pro-Carbide demonstration shortly after the leak. (Wide World Photos)

4

The Living Room Tragedy

Television critic Michael J. Arlen (1982) called Vietnam the living room war with some justification. Americans learned about Bhopal in much the same way—in the comfort of their armchairs and over dinner. But television's view of Bhopal was unique, for the portrait of the event painted by the print media was shaded and intensified by the added dimension of television's pictures and sharpened by the time constraints placed on the television medium. Those elements of the tragedy singled out by the print media for special examination were the subject of up-close and personal sorts of television coverage. Those events or issues which received secondary coverage in print reports were often missing from the small screen altogether.

But television inserted visual images into the message and repeated them often. Thus the words and pictures that made up the totality of television coverage provided a different view of Bhopal than that of the wire services, the newsmagazines and the prestige press. It was a view that, in some subtle sense, began to take on the aura of myth.

TELEVISION'S WORDS

Because the medium operates using both words and visual images, network Bhopal coverage was analyzed both in its component parts and as an entity. Taken by themselves, the words of television were similar to those in print, although the trends and tendencies of print media coverage were heightened in television reports.

First, television covered Bhopal as a human catastrophe. Its coverage was almost entirely event-oriented: Only 10.6 percent of the Bhopal stories broadcast on the three networks were aired during the month of January, and the vast majority of the television coverage, thirty-nine of forty-seven stories, was aired in the first two weeks after the event. Such timing indicates television coverage focused on the immediate events of Bhopal—the report of the incident, the suffering immediately afterward and Operation Faith—far more than any issue raised by the tragedy. Indeed, 46.3 percent of the television stories focused on the tragedy itself and the immediate aftermath, while similar incidents in other countries were the subject of only one (2.4 percent) television report. Union Carbide's response to the incident received the next largest share of television coverage—26.8 percent of the stories aired (eleven stories)—while stories focusing on the legal aftermath, all of which mentioned Union Carbide, comprised an additional 4.9 percent (two stories) of the coverage. Other topics were mentioned only briefly on television: The Indian government's response to the incident, 9.8 percent of the stories; and U.S. agency reports on the chemical industry or on specific inspections at the Institute plant, 4.9 percent. The fluctuating price of Union Carbide stock was the general topic of one (2.4 percent) report.

Since one of the primary criteria for reporting foreign news, at least as measured by media scholars, is loss of life and injury, it is not surprising that news of Bhopal—when it appeared on television—was among the top stories. Bhopal was one of the top three stories in the network newscasts 70.8 percent of the time Bhopal stories appeared, and it rated the number–one slot 22 percent of the time.

Not only did Bhopal receive top billing in many of the nightly newscasts, but television also gave the story import another way: In a medium where ninety seconds is considered a lengthy story, television provided extensive time to coverage of the tragedy. Of all the stories broadcast, 31.7 percent ran from two to three minutes in length, and an equal percentage, or thirteen stories, ran from three to five minutes. All the networks followed this trend providing what, by television standards, is a generous amount of air time to one particular event. Two of the networks went even further. NBC ran three Bhopal stories (20 percent of its coverage) of more than five minutes in length; ABC ran an identical number of five-minute-plus stories, a total of 23.1 percent of its reports.

Brief Bhopal stories definitely were not the rule, at least on the network news. ABC and NBC ran only one Bhopal story that lasted less than thiry seconds; CBS aired only two such stories. NBC carried one story that lasted between thirty and fifty-nine seconds, but neither of the other two networks aired such a piece. Only CBS ran a story of sixty–to ninety–second duration. The remainder of the coverage, on all three networks, was provided by more lengthy reports.

Despite its obvious links to events in the United States as well as other nations, television portrayed Bhopal as primarily an Indian tragedy. Sixty-one percent of the television news stories about the event used Bhopal itself as the primary focus of the report, while an additional 31.7 percent treated the events in Bhopal as a secondary focus. In contrast, only 2.4 percent of the television stories used Institute as a primary focus, while an additional 24.4 percent of the stories covered Institute as a secondary emphasis. More than half—61.0 percent of the television stories—did not mention the Bhopal-Institute connection.

While Institute did not serve as a major American link to the tragedy, television provided a different sort of "Americanization" of the story. About 12.2 percent of the Bhopal pieces included economic information—all of it focused on the continuing corporate health of Union Carbide.

This apparent inability to construe the story in its broadest scope, with the exception of the economic angle, was reflected in one additional way: The subject of technological hazards was the central focus of only one television report and the secondary focus of three others. More than 90 percent of the stories concerning Bhopal did not even mention the issue.

Television's emphasis on the event itself aided in producing another peculiarly televised view of Bhopal. Television reports portrayed the disaster as if it had happened largely outside an Indian historical and cultural context. There was no discussion of the economic problems and imperatives in India which had resulted in the construction of the Bhopal plant and the more recent financial pressures on it. Only one story contained some explanation of Indian cultural patterns, for example, the mushrooming of slums around the plant, and how the growth of the shantytowns contributed to some aspects of the tragedy.

In television's view, the significance of the event was in the number of dead and injured. This "body count" emphasis was apparent in a number of ways. All the television coverage centered on two phases of the event. First, 34.1 percent of the reports focused on the immediate disaster impact—the original body count. The remaining 65.9 percent of the stories centered on some rehabilitation and recovery issues: Operation Faith—would the body count climb?; the impact the Bhopal tragedy might have on the Indian elections—would Rajiv Gandhi survive?; the long-term legal and economic battles that were likely to result—would Union Carbide survive?

The human statistics did not become a base from which to examine more global and long-term issues. Only one television story focused on the long-term health impact of the event, although nine other stories included discussion of the long-term health consequences as a secondary focus.

The legal wrangling over the disaster was the primary focus of two stories. However, the networks were scrupulously careful to avoid attributing any blame for the incident. Almost all the television stories—92.7 percent—did not include a specific statement of blame other than those attributed to various people, primarily lawyers, interviewed on videotape.

However, when all was said and watched, 70 percent of the network coverage contained no discussion of the long-term health, environmental, social or legal issues the Bhopal tragedy raised.

Television's ability to connect its audience to the disaster appeared to be housed in the qualities of the small screen itself and in the potency of a picture of a suffering man, woman or child. Thus, television provided a significantly more in-depth portrait of one aspect of the tragedy: personalization of Bhopal's victims. More than one-third of the stories, 36.6 percent, identified individual victims in the script as well as through images on videotape. But the networks were not consistent in this presentation: ABC personified individual victims in 61.5 percent of its story scripts, NBC in 40 percent of its story scripts, but CBS in only 7.7 percent of its written reports.

This singular difference, however, does not offset the general sameness of the television coverage. Those Americans who received all of their news about Bhopal from the television networks were told of a far-away event, bereft of long-term consequences, larger issues which might have applications in their own lives and the social, economic and cultural background which would enable them to discover a well-integrated meaning in the Bhopal disaster. In place of this more integrated understanding was an emphasis on human suffering—but without the contextual connection.

TELEVISION'S VIEW OF THE NEWS

Categorization can reveal some important trends—but it does not provide a complete picture, particularly of television news. Much of what the networks do may be ascribed to their various competitive positions, to the history of relatively strong or weak news organizations and to the abilities of individual reporters and videographers. So despite the lack of statistical differences between the networks, each covered the Bhopal story in a slightly different way.

During the first week of the tragedy, NBC viewers saw the flabbiest coverage of the event. The network was scooped by both CBS and ABC on significant aspects of the story. In addition, NBC's coverage relied on the general and on generalizations more than the coverage provided by the other networks. Specific facts and figures about some important "episodes" in the Bhopal event were absent from NBC reports during that first week, although the network did a somewhat better job of providing information about the long-term health effects of the leak.

The factual kudos during the first day of coverage belonged to ABC. Not only did the network report a precise death and injury count—something that was lacking on NBC—but it also was the only network to report the suspension of MIC production at Institute. CBS, while missing this key element of the

Bhopal story that day, did provide viewers with some important background information on why the plant had been built in India. NBC's report lacked specific death and injury figures, news of the arrests of workers at the plant in connection with the leak and word that MIC production at Institute had been suspended. All three networks, however, carried Union Carbide's response to the disaster.

The pattern set by the first day's coverage was repeated throughout the remainder of the week, when Bhopal was the top story on all three networks almost every day. NBC was forced to play catch-up. It reported the suspension of production in Institute on December 4 as part of a larger segment outlining the dangers chemical manufacturing posed in the Kanawah Valley. The second day's NBC report also included some of the most clichéd writing of the television coverage, describing Institute as a "gritty little petrochemical town."

However, in an effort to camouflage its weak first–day reports, NBC led its December 4 coverage with discussion of the medical implications of the event—a portion of the story the network emphasized throughout its coverage.

CBS followed a similar pattern because it, too, had been scooped on the Institute suspension. The network devoted a major portion of its Bhopal report to coverage of Institute, background on the Institute plant and the community's fear. ABC, while also carrying news of Institute, chose to emphasize the events in Bhopal itself, including updates on the dead and injured, a segment on medical problems and relief efforts and a scientific report on MIC and what was known about its toxic properties.

Again, ABC scooped the other two networks on the second day of coverage; it was the first to report that a team of Union Carbide scientists had been sent to Bhopal to investigate the accident and to aid in the relief efforts.

Third-day coverage on all three networks emphasized the toll of dead and injured and the increasingly apparent medical problems caused by the leak. NBC led its broadcast with the report that there was "a death a minute" in Bhopal while CBS opened with a death and injury toll update augmented by reports of the problems corpse disposal was causing. ABC almost seemed to apologize for placing the story at the head of the newscast. Peter Jennings, at the opening of the Bhopal segment, told viewers "it is the ever increasing dimension of that tragedy in Bhopal, India, that puts this story once again at the top of our broadcast."

While NBC stuck almost exclusively to a focus on the dead and injured, the CBS report for December 5 also included a scientific story on the toxic properties of MIC and a report that there was no known antidote to the chemical. ABC had already carried such a report; NBC never really provided much detailed scientific information about the gas.

CBS also was the first network to focus on the regulatory issues the tragedy raised. The regulatory angle was addressed only obliquely on ABC that day when Jennings interviewed Carbide corporate spokesman Jackson Browning and asked him who should be held responsible for the leak. Jennings's questions, while probing, also gave Browning the opportunity to note that the Bhopal plant originally had been built far from a population center, a point not made on the other two networks.

Despite some good reporting, however, ABC on December 5 made the first significant error of its coverage when it reported widespread blindness due to the leak. Not only was the report itself exaggerated—there were temporary vision problems but no permanent blindness attributed to the leak—but correct information was not broadcast until December 15. But the correct account appeared on CBS.

NBC filed the most detailed report of December 6, but much of the information in it—for example, reports of blindness, background information on why India needed a home-grown pesticide industry and questions about regulation—had been carried on the other networks. However, NBC concluded its story with a report of an MIC leak near an American elementary school about six months before the Bhopal disaster. No one was injured, although some teachers and students were treated and sent home. Neither of the other networks picked up the story, although AP ran a similar report.

That day all three networks featured the arrival of the Union Carbide team in India and the initial filing of various suits. CBS and ABC also focused on the return home of some Bhopal survivors, a shift in emphasis that carried through the remainder of the television coverage.

By week's end, December 7, the network reports differed in only minor ways. All three, for example, reported Anderson's arrest, although only NBC had actual footage of Anderson after his release. Both ABC and CBS listed the precise charges the Indian government had filed against Anderson, a detail NBC omitted. Both CBS and ABC tried to report on the reasons "behind" Anderson's arrest. CBS raised the question of a hidden Indian agenda, but the ABC report concluded Anderson had been detained to allow the local Indian state government to avoid appearing helpless.

NBC was the only network to report that the Indian government apparently had deliberately deflated death and injury figures to avoid panic. The video aired during this NBC segment was one of few which did not precisely match the reporter's words. NBC aired only photographs of victims—as opposed to government officials—when it reported the government inaccuracies.

NBC was the only network with a national newscast on December 8, and the report was primarily an update of the previous week's events. It included new death toll figures, mention of the beginning of the Union Carbide investigation, further discussion of the long–term health problems associated with the leak and photographs of lawyer Melvin Belli arriving in India.

Both NBC and ABC carried reports the next day. On December 9 NBC led with the rising death toll and continuing medical problems while ABC began with Anderson's return to the United States. Medical problems were the secondary emphasis in the ABC report, while NBC placed its secondary emphasis on Institute, including reports of the unemployment problem there, public hearings on safety, and the area's evacuation plans. ABC chose to focus on the larger issue of technological hazard through coverage of Department of Defense research in Cambridge. The network used perhaps the most unusual video in all the television coverage during this Sunday report: It broadcast newsreel footage of soldiers being gassed during the trench warfare of World War I to open its technological hazard segment.

By the beginning of the second regular week of coverage, the networks were running almost identical stories.

On December 10, NBC reported—without citing specifics—the 1982 Carbide study of the safety conditions in the Bhopal plant. Anderson was quoted as saying victims would be fairly and adequately compensated, and the identical quote was used on the other two networks. From there, NBC focused on the economic impact the disaster was having on Union Carbide, including the declining value of its stock and the suits being filed against the corporation. In what may have been a move to provoke a public response similar to that generated after the network's powerful breaking of the Ethiopian famine story about two months earlier, NBC closed its Monday newscast by noting, "And Indian officials have made it clear they would welcome help from foreign countries, either from governments or from private individuals."

That same day CBS and ABC both focused on the legal implications of the leak, although both led with Bhopal updates. CBS noted Bhopal's air and water had been declared safe, while ABC reported eleven more people had died. CBS painted a caustic—and no doubt intentional—report of the deluge of American lawyers, noting: "On the heels of these (funeral) processions came a procession of American lawyers adding up the losses to sue for compensation." ABC's report included a segment on the heroic actions of an Indian railway worker who refused to leave his post at the height of the leak, thus saving many lives.

But, with these exceptions, the overall content of the news reports remained the same—the networks were updating and backgrounding, waiting for additional events to break.

They did on December 11, when both NBC and ABC led their reports with coverage of the first tour of the Institute plant Carbide had allowed since the accident. All three networks carried footage of Mother Teresa's visit to Bhopal, and all three began to address directly the issue of blame, although in different ways. NBC reported Union Carbide officials suggesting the blame for the leak should be placed with Carbide officials in India and cited corporate documents outlining differences in the safety systems between the Institute and Bhopal plants. CBS addressed the blame issue through a segment on Carbide's "open" public relations strategy; ABC told its viewers an Indian journalist had warned about the potential for disaster at the Bhopal plant six months before the leak.

However, there was an important distinction among the network reports that day. NBC did not report Carbide was planning to neutralize the remaining MIC in Bhopal, a fact which appeared near the top of the CBS newscast and which appeared near the kicker in the ABC report.

By the next day all three networks had picked up on the importance of the neutralization plans. Each led with the story. The reports, however, differed on how many people had fled the city. NBC reported 125,000 people had evacuated, CBS 100,000 and ABC provided no exact figure. NBC also reported that thirty tons of MIC would be neutralized. At the same time, the print media were reporting about fifteen tons of the substance would be disposed of. While the initial television reports thus seemed to include a rather gross error, when Operation Faith concluded about twenty-two to twenty-four tons of MIC had been neutralized. Thus the television reports appear to have been as much in error, although in a different direction, than similar initial reports in print.

The three networks focused almost exclusively on Operation Faith—the neutralization effort—and the flight from Bhopal in stories on December 13, with ABC providing a few more details. A similar pattern prevailed the next day. All three networks aired videotape of Anderson saying, "I think Bhopal has changed the world," at the public hearing before a U.S. House subcommittee held in Institute. Both NBC and ABC also reported the contents of 1981 EPA documents which detailed the number and amount of various chemical leaks in the Institute plant. The issue of government regulation of the chemical industry was raised in both CBS and ABC reports.

Over the weekend—December 15 and 16—Operation Faith dominated the news. NBC did not air a national news show. CBS on December 15, and ABC and CBS the following day, devoted almost all their coverage to the neutralization process, some discussion of the long–term health impact of the disaster— including the correction of the reports of blindness—and some coverage of the regulation debate that was beginning to take place in Washington.

Reports the following Monday were almost identical and focused on the near completion of Operation Faith. All the networks reported the work was half done when, in fact, because technicians were finding additional MIC in the tanks, it was not. All three also reported the return of some survivors to the city. Monday was the last day (during the study period) that all three networks devoted some time to Bhopal coverage. The event surfaced briefly on December 26 and 29 on NBC in coverage of the Indian elections, and in a report about the unloading of the MIC which had been refused by Brazil at Norfolk, Virginia, and its subsequent shipment to Woodbine, Georgia.

These network-by-network comparisons, while subjective, flesh out the statistical portrait. There were some minor scoops, as well as some fact errors, which, in the larger scheme of the events of Bhopal, are not significant for the impact of the overall story. The network newscasts played Bhopal very much as an event—with little mention of the larger issues of technological hazards except as viewers chose to "read them into" network reports.

But video expands television coverage in sometimes unforeseen ways, and in the Bhopal story, the video coverage itself began to hint at a deeper meaning, one which focused not so much on technological hazard as on society's way of dealing with the foreboding a technological error produces in the culture at large.

TELEVISION'S PICTURES

Television does not function by words alone. Indeed, scholars who study how it is that human beings learn and remember know most people learn through a combination of what they see as well as what they read. Television has learned to utilize that sensory edge, for it brings information to the viewing public primarily through the eye and the ear, with only secondary information left to be "read" on the screen.

Network news coverage in the 1980s emphasizes nothing so

much as the visual. The talking head—the anchor reading a story with only a blank screen or map of the world in view behind him—is a thing of the medium's past. Indeed, this reliance on the visual provided television with one of the first hurdles it had to overcome in reporting the story: Bhopal, India, was so far away that December 3 coverage on all three networks carried not a single second of footage from the relatively remote location. But distance didn't halt the visual imperative. The networks compensated throughout their coverage, often in unusual and sometimes in creative and artistic ways.

In all the Bhopal coverage, no anchor was allowed to be a talking head. Almost three-fourths (73.2 percent) of the network news stories combined the use of the anchor, at least one graphic, videotape and a reporter "standup"—that is, a reporter introducing or closing a story with the locale, as opposed to a studio, visible in the background. An additional 19.5 percent of the networks' Bhopal stories combined the use of a studio anchor, at least one graphic plus videotape, while 7.3 percent of the stories broadcast relied on the anchor, videotape and a reporter-in-the-field standup.

The videotape itself, which carried the bulk of the visual images on the television screen, oriented viewers to the human magnitude of the immediate events of the Bhopal disaster. And television's coverage, while it carried pictures of Carbide spokesmen, Mother Teresa and representatives from both the Indian and the United States governments—plus the occasional doctor or scientist—also focused on the dead and the living victims of Bhopal.

—While 68.3 percent of the stories did not include footage of the dead, burial sites or funeral pyres, in the remaining 31.7 percent of the stories there were sixty-nine separate such images.

—The vast majority—80.5 percent—of television stories did not include images of dead children. But in the stories that did present such pictures, there were twenty such separate images. Eleven of those images were in close-up where the child's face or the shroud over the face was clearly visible.

—Living children were portrayed as victims of the Bhopal disaster in two-fifths—41.5 percent—of the stories. Fifty-one separate images of living children as victims were used in those segments, thirty-seven of them in close–up.

—More than half of the television news reports—53.7 percent—included shots of women as victims, either living or dead. Forty-six such separate images were presented, twenty-eight of them in close–up. Men were portrayed as victims, either living or dead, in the same number of reports, 53.7 percent. Seventy-one separate images of men as victims were aired during those segments, including forty close–up shots.

This is not to say that such images are in any way untruthful, for part of the tragedy of the Bhopal disaster was the number of dead and injured. But because television chose to highlight the immediate events of what was a lengthy and complicated story, its video coverage naturally focused on the most dramatic and vivid witnesses to what had gone wrong.

While videotape carried the bulk of the visual message, the visual emphasis began from the first second of every Bhopal story. In only three network reports was the anchor allowed to deliver his lead-in without the support of a background graphic. Forty-one percent of the stories used just one graphic during Bhopal reports, but 26.8 percent of the stories required two different graphics, and 19.5 percent used three separate drawings, animated drawings or, occasionally, still photographs as graphics. One network story used four different graphics; one other story used five.

The networks often used graphics to orient the reader to the story itself or to particular events within the story. Thus the most popular graphic was a map of India noting the location of Bhopal. The second most popular graphic was a map of India without noting the specific site of the tragedy. In stories where only one graphic was used the Union Carbide logo was the third most popular choice—7.3 percent of the stories used it—followed by still photographs of the victims and still photographs of Union Carbide officials, each used in 4.9 percent of the stories. A map of West Virginia was used as the first graphic in 2.4 percent (one story) and miscellaneous graphics were used in 12.2 percent (five stories) of the network reports.

The pattern of using graphics to allow viewers to locate events geographically continued with stories in which two graphics were used. The most popular "second" graphic used by the networks was a map of West Virginia, 14.6 percent, while the Union Carbide logo was used as a second graphic 12.2 percent of the time. Still photographs of Union Carbide officials were used 4.9 percent of the time while animated graphics illustrating "what happened inside the plant" were used as second graphics once.

The geographic orientation consensus vanished when three graphics were used. Still photographs of the victims were the most frequently used third graphic, appearing 17.1 percent of the time in stories in which three graphics were used. The Union Carbide logo, still photographs of Union Carbide officials and animated drawings of "what happened inside the plant" each were used 2.4 percent (once) in such stories.

The emphasis on telling the story through the suffering of individual human beings and using pictures to orient viewers both geographically and to subject matter was predictable. But television added one additional image of Bhopal to the American video vocabulary. Television footage of Bhopal became synonymous with gas—and the networks and their videographers created a number of ways to portray it. Smokestacks—particularly in the background—were common currency among pictures of Institute and Bhopal. Several of the graphics used by the networks included static or animated clouds of gas. One network, ABC, tucked in old newsreel footage of soldiers in World War I trench fighting—wearing gas masks. In all 68.3 percent of the television stories about Bhopal included an image of gas, and those 28 stories contained 115 separate images of gas or of objects like smokestacks which were either producing some sort of emission on camera or could be considered as capable of producing emissions.

The prevalence and sheer number of these images of gas, while not necessarily conscious on the part of photographers or reporters who needed good background for their standups, became inextricable from Bhopal itself. In some symbolic ways, the ever-present gas images came to represent the larger issues of Bhopal, and to add subtly to the cultural meaning which any worldwide disaster creates and shapes.

5

Patterns of Power

A MEDIATED VIEW OF AUTHORITY

If media coverage were a gauge of reality, then institutions, and those who represented them, were the people with power in the Bhopal catastrophe. Whether it was reflected in the sources most frequently cited by the various media outlets covering the events, those people who were portrayed as powerful actors within the various stories, or the overall impression of "help-lessness" the reports conveyed, institutions—particularly corporate and government institutions—were portrayed as possessing some understanding of or ability to alter events in Bhopal.

An overview of all media reports reflected this bias in a number of ways. First, as good reporting practice dictates, confirmation of fact and opinion was lodged in story sources. About 47 percent of the stories analyzed included citation either of one, two or three separate sources of information, and an additional 9.6 percent of the stories included a specific citation of at least four sources. About 10.7 percent of the articles printed or broadcast cited nine or more separate sources. Contrary to past research, only 10.2 percent of the Bhopal stories included no source citation. Most such stories were editorials, letters to the editor or news summaries and thus would not be expected to include source citations comparable to news reports.

So, while it would appear the news media had a vast number

of opportunities to deliver facts and opinions about events in Bhopal, the pool of sources actually used was a relatively restricted one. The two most frequently cited sources were named Union Carbide officials in the United States (10 percent, with anonymous U.S. Union Carbide officials cited an additional 2.8 percent of the time) and named American government officials, 10.8 percent. The Indian news media was the third most frequently cited source, 7.6 percent.

By contrast, regardless of nationality, doctors or scientists were cited as sources less than 7 percent of the time. The "unknowns"—the Indian workers at the Bhopal plant and the average American citizen—were cited less than 2 percent of the time.

In general, the number of types of sources cited indicated that the news media covered this highly complex and technical story in much the same way as more traditional stories are reported— relying on government and corporate officials for the bulk of information and turning to less traditional, although arguably more knowledgeable, sources less frequently.

The same pattern persisted when it came to those institutions or people the media portrayed as powerful actors, those who had the ability somehow to alter events, in the Bhopal disaster. Union Carbide as a corporation (11 percent) and American business executives, including Union Carbide corporate officials (11 percent), were the two entities most frequently portrayed as powerful actors in media reports. In 44 percent of the stories Americans, either as lawyers, corporate executives or corporations, were portrayed as the most powerful actors on the scene. Indians were portrayed as powerful actors only 2.8 percent of the time, and the bulk of that coverage focused on Indian government officials. Individuals, particularly Indians who were not officials of their own government or of Union Carbide of India, Ltd., were not portrayed as capable of influencing events. Instead, they became masses of victims.

This emphasis on the institutional—in conjunction with the media's tendency to report Bhopal as a discrete, unpredictable event disconnected from history, culture and economics—may have contributed to yet another characteristic of the media reports: an overall tone of mild helplessness. About 29.9 percent

of the stories analyzed conveyed an impression of mild helplessness and an additional 21.4 percent of the reports conveyed
a tone of extreme helplessness. While a tone of helplessness was
judged irrelevant in 30.3 percent of the reports—and one could
reasonably argue that some reflection of helplessness would be
little more than accurate in a disaster such as the one in Bhopal—
the great majority of media reports conveyed the sense that there
was little that could have altered the events.

Different media, of course, treated these various issues somewhat differently. Those differences, too, raise some intriguing
questions about the shaping of a media culture of disasters.

THE NUMBER OF SOURCES

As previously indicated, research of media coverage of hazards during the 1960s found that many media reports did not
include specific source citations. Such was not the case in Bhopal
coverage. In fact, even those outlets traditionally criticized for
citing few sources—primarily television—often cited multiple
sources in Bhopal reports.

No national television network story about Bhopal was broadcast without the citation of at least one specific source. However,
14.6 percent of the television network reports included the citation of only one source, and 34.3 percent of the network stories
relied on three or fewer sources. Thus multiple sources were
the rule rather than the exception of network coverage. Four to
eight sources were cited in 48.9 percent of the television reports,
and 17.1 percent of the network stories incorporated nine or
more sources. The networks did not differ from each other in
the number of sources cited in a statistically significant fashion,
although in percentage terms ABC tended to use a higher number of sources—nine or more per story—than did CBS or NBC.
At least when it came to Bhopal coverage, the days of the
"sourceless" television report appeared to be over.

The wires followed a similar pattern with one important exception—5.5 percent of the wire service reports did not include
specific source citations. Some of the these "sourceless" reports,
however, were news summaries, which do not always include
specific source citations and which generally refer to longer and

more detailed articles. About 18.7 percent of the wire reports relied on only one source, and almost half, 49 percent, of the wire stories relied on one, two or three cited sources of information. In this sense, the wires relied on relatively fewer specific sources than did the television networks. However, the relatively small number of television reports compared to the literally hundreds of wire stories mean that any firm conclusions to be drawn from that direct comparison must be carefully qualified. In addition, 35.7 percent of the wire accounts relied on citation of from four to eight sources, and 9.8 percent of the wire reports included nine or more different sources of information.

There was, however, some statistical distinction between the wires (Chi square = .0001). Of the 214 AP reports, only four failed to include any source citation—1.9 percent of all the stories AP ran. In contrast, UPI's coverage included 20 of 177 stories (11.3 percent) without a source citation, and Reuters's coverage included 3.8 percent (5 of 132 stories) without a specific source. The Associated Press's reports, to a greater extent than the other two wires, included a relatively higher number of stories with many sources. AP's coverage included thirty stories (14.0 percent) for which nine or more sources were used. Similar coverage in UPI amounted to only 4.5 percent of its reports while Reuters stood midway between the two American services with 9.8 percent (thirteen stories) citing nine or more different sources.

Magazine coverage, because it is expected to be in more depth, might logically be expected to include a greater number of sources in its reports. However, such was not the case in Bhopal reports. If letters to the editor—which generally do not include a specific source citation but are rather a reflection of the author's opinions—were excluded, then the bulk of all magazine reports, 64.4 percent, included the citation of from one to eight sources. However, the magazines were significantly different from each other in how they "sourced" their stories. *Time*, which published the most letters to the editor, also published the greatest number of stories (five) which relied on nine or more sources. *Newsweek* and *U.S. News & World Report*, on the other hand, used from one to eight sources in 60 and 75 percent of their articles, respectively. *Newsweek* ran only three Bhopal stories which cited nine or more sources and *U.S. News* ran only one such story. In terms of percentages, this reliance on many sources by the newsmagazines equals or exceeds the performance by the wires. However, in terms of expectations, and the conventional wisdom of the journalistic profession, the newsmagazines relied on fewer distinct sources than might have been expected.

The performance by the prestige press mirrored that of the wires. Relatively few stories, only 5.8 percent (thirteen articles) were without a source, and most of these were letters to the editor or editorials. On the other end of the source continuum, 14.5 percent of the *New York Times* articles cited nine or more different sources while 12.3 percent of the *Washington Post* reports did so. The vast majority of stories in both papers, 80.7 percent in the *Times* and 78.9 percent in the *Post*, used from one to eight separate sources. There was no statistically significant difference between the two publications in this area.

Thus, when it came to reporting events in Bhopal, the mass media did cite sources—multiple sources in the vast majority of the news coverage. This willingness to state where information came from, at least in Bhopal reports, should do much to assuage criticism that the mass media too often publish or air news accounts without specific source citation. However, the kinds of sources the mass media cited raise a different set of questions, one which may give critics a different view of the institutions the various media outlets represent.

AUTHORITY AS SOURCE

At least as far as television was concerned, news of Bhopal was best conveyed by government or Union Carbide officials. The three most frequently cited sources in television news reports fell into those two categories, and collectively the two governments involved and Union Carbide comprised more than 50 percent of the top three sources cited in television news reports.

The two most frequently cited sources in television news reports were government officials, either from the United States or India (40.0 percent), and Union Carbide officials in the United States or India (32.5 percent). NBC and CBS relied more heavily on government sources—46.2 percent and 41.7 percent, respectively—than did ABC, which used a government official as the most frequently cited source in 33.3 percent of its reports. Union Carbide officials, however, were the most frequently cited source on that network; ABC cited Union Carbide officials as sources of first choice in 46.7 percent of its reports. Taken together, the two groups accounted for 72.5 percent of the most frequently cited television sources, leaving other groups far in the background. Citizens, either Indians or Americans, were the most frequently cited source in 10 percent of the television reports. The news media, primarily the Indian news media, also were the most frequently cited source in 10 percent of the television reports. Scientists and doctors fared even less well, appearing as the most frequently cited source in only 7.5 percent of the television reports. Ironically, attorneys were heard from not at all—at least as the most frequently cited television source.

However, since television relied on multiple sources, the pattern revealed by the analysis of the most frequently cited source does not provide a complete portrait. Analysis of the second and third most frequently cited sources in television news stories provided some variation, particularly the emergence of doctors, scientists and citizens as sources of some note.

The second most frequently cited source in television news reports was Union Carbide officials, either in this country or in India (33.3 percent). Government officials were the second most frequently cited source in an additional 26.7 percent of the television news stories. These two groups thus comprised 60 percent of the second most frequently cited sources in television news.

However, citizens, who were seldom visible as the most frequently cited television news source, were the second most frequently cited source in an additional 23.3 percent of the reports. Scientists or doctors and the news media were the second most frequently cited source 6.7 percent of the time. Attorneys, who were never the most frequently cited source in television reports, were the second most frequently cited source 3.3 percent of the time in television coverage.

Government officials continued to dominate television sourcing when the third most frequently cited source was analyzed.

Government officials, either in India or in the United States, were the third most frequently cited source 32.3 percent of the time. However, scientists and doctors were the third most frequently cited source in 22.6 percent of the television reports while Union Carbide officials were the third most frequently cited source only 16.1 percent of the time. The average Indian or American citizen was the third most frequently cited source 12.9 percent of the time in television news reports, while the news media, primarily the Indian news media, was the third most frequently cited source in 9.7 percent of the television reports. Attorneys functioned as the third most frequently cited source 6.5 percent of the time.

Since most of the television news coverage cited either one, two or three sources, this reliance on institutional sources— either government or corporate—takes on additional weight. However, citizens did have some role in television news reports, a pattern that was not widely copied in the print media, and doctors and scientists emerged as an important secondary source in a story with obvious scientifc and medical components. Perhaps what is most surprising is the number of times the television news media cited other news outlets as a source of information. Such a bias reflects not only a reliance on institutions but also the handicap distance and a foreign country place on television news. Television reports relied to an important degree on Indian coverage of the tragedy to complete the picture presented to American viewers.

THE SOURCE OF WIRE REPORTS

The wire service followed the same sourcing patterns as television news with two important exceptions: the reliance on government sources of information was even more pronounced, and scientists, doctors and citizens never really emerged as dominant information sources. There were no statistically significant differences among the wire services in their sourcing patterns.

More than two-fifths, 41.5 percent, of the wire service reports named government officials as the most frequently cited source of information on Bhopal. An additional one-fifth of wire service reports, 20.8 percent, relied on Union Carbide officials, and sometimes company documents, as the most frequently cited source. Thus, just as did the television reports, the wire services relied on these two institutions—one corporate and one governmental—as the dominant information source in Bhopal reports.

The next most frequently cited wire service source was the news media itself, which was the most frequently cited source in 15 percent of the reports. The vast majority of these citations were to the Indian news media, primarily the India wire services but occasionally specific stories in specific publications. Attorneys were the most frequently cited source in 10 percent of the wire reports. Scientists and citizens were given even less play, functioning as the most frequently cited source only 8.5 and 4.2 percent of the time, respectively.

This basic pattern with little change persisted in the second and third most frequently cited sources in wire services reports.

Goverment officials were the second most frequently cited source 43.9 percent of the time in wire reports, and the third most frequently cited source 36.6 percent of the time. In both instances, no group was cited more often by the wires than officials from the American or Indian governments. Union Carbide officials also continued to dominate the list of most frequently cited sources. Carbide was the second most frequently cited source in 24.6 percent of the wire reports and the third most frequently cited source in 20.1 percent of the wire coverage. Again, these two institutions accounted for more than half of the second and third most frequently cited sources in the wires' Bhopal coverage.

The news media itself also continued to play a central role in providing information to the wires. About 11 percent of the wire reports listed news organizations as the second most frequently cited source; that reliance rose to 13.6 percent in the analysis of the third most frequently cited source.

Citizens, attorneys and scientists and doctors lagged far behind, at least as far as the wires were concerned. Scientists or doctors were the second most frequently cited source in 7.5 percent of the wire reports, and they served as the third most frequently cited source in 9.2 percent of the reports. Attorneys were the second most frequently cited source 6.9 percent of the time and the third most frequently cited source in 7.3 percent of the wire reports.

Only citizens functioned as increasingly more important sources when the second and third most frequently cited sources were analyzed. The average citizen, either Indian or American, was the second most frequently cited source in 5.5 percent of the wire reports, but the third most frequently cited source in 13.2 percent of the wire reports.

Once again, the media pattern of relying on official and relatively easily accessible sources from institutions and the corporate world was apparent in wire service coverage. Scientists and doctors played a much more secondary role, as did the citizens whose lives were changed by the events.

THE PRESTIGE PRESS CITES THE PRESTIGIOUS

The sourcing pattern in the prestige press fell somewhat between the pattern and variations established by television and wire service reports, with no statistically significant variation between the *Times* and the *Post*. Government officials dominated the sources cited in prestige press reports, followed by Union Carbide officials and the news media themselves. Citizens and scientists played a somewhat greater role in prestige press reports, although not to the same degree as in television coverage. Attorneys, in the prestige press, were the least frequently cited of the various source groups.

Unlike television and wire service reports, the prestige press did not use institutional sources 60 percent of the time when the most frequently cited source was analyzed. That mediated reliance dropped to only 50 percent. Government officials were the most frequently cited source in 28.6 percent of the reports by the *Times* and the *Post*; Union Carbide officials were the most frequently cited sources in an additional 22.8 percent of the time.

However, scientists were the most frequently cited source in 16.1 percent of the prestige press reports—the most dominant use of scientists as the most frequently cited source of any of the media outlets studied. Citizens also were cited more frequently in prestige press reports. In fact, they were the most frequently cited source in 14.9 percent of the coverage provided by the *Post* and the *Times*.

This subtle shift in emphasis—at least in terms of the most frequently cited source—meant that the news media itself played a somewhat less dominant role as a source in prestige press reports. Other news organizations were the most frequently cited source in 9.3 percent of prestige press reports; attorneys were the most frequently cited source in 8.7 percent of the stories.

This somewhat distinct distribution of sources, however, did not continue in the second and third most frequently cited sources of prestige press reports. On that level of analysis government officials, and to a somewhat lesser extent Union Carbide officials, took on an increasingly dominant role as information sources.

Government officials, either in the United States or in India, were the second most frequently cited sources in 35.0 percent of the prestige press reports and the third most frequently cited source in 37.9 percent of the reports. Union Carbide officials were the second most frequently cited source in 31.4 percent of the reports, but the third most frequently cited source in only 19 percent of the reports.

These shifts may reflect the *Post*'s reporting of the Bhopal story as a political story, for the paper relied on government officials at least one-third of the time as the most frequently cited source, as well as the second and the third most frequently cited source. The *Times*, by contrast, cited government officials at least one-third of the time only in the third most frequently cited source analysis. However, these percentage differences were not reflected in more exacting measures of statistical significance.

Scientists were the most frequently cited source in 10 percent of the prestige press coverage and the third most frequently cited source in 8.6 percent of the reports. Citizens, however, were the second most frequently cited source in only 7.1 percent of the prestige press reports, although they became the third most frequently cited source in 17.2 percent of the stories. The *Post* relied more on citizens as sources than did the *Times* in the second and third most frequently cited source analysis. Again, such sourcing may have reflected the *Post*'s greater coverage of Institute, although the percentage differences were not reflected in more stringent statistical tests.

The prestige press apparently did not place as great a reliance on other news organizations, particularly Indian news organizations, as did the other media outlets studied. The news media were the second most frequently cited source in 9.3 percent of the prestige press reports and the third most frequently cited source in 12.9 percent of those reports.

Finally, despite the coverage of the legal aspects of the Bhopal story, attorneys themselves were not prominent sources in the prestige press. Lawyers, either Indian or American, were the second most frequently cited source in 8.7 percent of the prestige press reports; they were the third most frequently cited source in 7.1 percent of the stories.

The sources cited by the three newsmagazines proved exceptional only because the pattern defied conventional wisdom. While the magazines might have been expected to provide more in-depth coverage, the three publications accomplished that goal by citing the same sorts of sources favored by the wire services and the prestige press. While there were percentage differences among the three publications, those differences did not meet more stringent tests for statistical significance.

The most frequently cited source, in two of the three publications, was government officials, either in India or the United States. Those same officials were the second most frequently cited source in all three publications, 36.6 percent of the sources cited, and the third most frequently cited in all three magazines almost as often—31.3 percent.

U.S. News & World Report provided the only exception: Its most frequently cited source was individual citizens, who were the most frequently cited sources in 33.3 percent of its ten stories, followed by government officials, attorneys, Union Carbide corporate officials and other news organizations, each of which functioned as the most frequently cited source in *U.S. News* 16.7 percent of the time.

Newsweek and *Time* followed the already apparent pattern. The news media were the most frequently cited source in 27.3 and 11 percent of the two publications' reports, respectively, and

Union Carbide officials or corporate documents were the most frequently cited source 18.2 and 22.2 percent of the time, respectively.

While the pattern of "most frequently cited source" used by the magazines was somewhat atypical, the second and third most frequently cited sources conformed more to the emerging pattern. Government sources took and maintained a dominant role followed by corporate sources, the second most frequently cited source 27.3 percent of the time in magazine stories. Here again, *U.S. News* pitched itself on the outer end of the continuum: Union Carbide officials functioned as the second most frequently cited source in 60 percent of the publication's reports—a percentage unequalled by any other medium studied. Union Carbide officials functioned as the third most frequently cited source in *U.S. News* an additional 20 percent of the time. Such a reliance on Carbide as a story source also suggests the sort of story the magazine told: one of corporate impact rather than a more "news–and event–" oriented view.

Although the magazines provided more issue-oriented coverage than the other print media, they did not do so through quoting scientists and citizens. Scientists were the most frequently cited source in only 11.5 percent of the magazine reports—one story in *Time* and two articles in *Newsweek* but in none of the *U.S. News* stories. Nor did the newsmagazines rely more on scientists as the second and third most frequently cited sources. Scientists and doctors were the second most frequently cited source in two reports (9.1 percent of the total coverage), one in *Time* and another in *Newsweek*, and the third most frequently cited source in only one report, that in *U.S. News* (6.3 percent of the magazine's reports).

Citizens appeared more frequently, serving as the most frequently cited source in 15.4 percent of the magazine reports (four articles), 9.1 percent of the time as the second most frequently cited source (two stories), and 18.1 percent of the time (three articles) as the third most frequently cited source.

Attorneys, too, lagged far behind. They were the most frequently cited source in only two reports, 7.7 percent of the magazine coverage, the second most frequently cited source in one article in each of the three publications (13.6 percent of the magazine coverage) and the third most frequently cited source in two reports, or 12.5 percent of the coverage.

Magazine coverage, although it was more issue–oriented, focused on those issues relying on the same sorts of sources as the other print media. Whether additional depth could truly be gained from such a sourcing pattern is debatable: Government officials quoted at length certainly could have added both breadth and detail to the story. But the fact that scientists and doctors, as well as citizens who were affected or could have been affected, were consulted so infrequently also suggests that the depth the magazines may have provided was in a traditional vein. Political conflict over rules and regulations was, in some sense, substituted for the discussion of scientific and technical issues which form the infrastructure of the political debate.

Thus, while there were some minor variations, the mass media's emphasis on official and easily accessible sources pervaded Bhopal coverage regardless of news organization. Scientists and doctors, and to an even smaller degree individual citizens, had little visible role to play, although television and the prestige press provided citizens themselves with more visibility—often as victims—than did the wires. Such an institutional emphasis was predictable, although for such a complex story media critics and those who are concerned with hazard mitigation might have hoped to find a more diverse pattern of information collection.

However, in the information age, information means power; and the patterns of power in the mediated portrait of Bhopal were not confined strictly to the sources the various news organizations cited.

THE POWERFUL ACTORS

When it came to those who were portrayed as having the power to alter or direct the events that comprised the Bhopal tragedy, the news media provided one view: Institutions were far more powerful than individuals, and Americans were far more powerful than Indians. Whether it was television, the newsmagazines, the prestige press or the three wire services, the power constellation remained the same. To be a powerful actor in the Bhopal tragedy, it was necessary to be an institution or to represent one. Others simply couldn't compete.

In television coverage, the most powerful actor in the stories was an institution—generally a government or a corporation— 42.9 percent of the time. Those who watched NBC saw institutions portrayed as powerful actors in 54.5 percent of the network's reports; CBS viewers were treated to that view 45.5 percent of the time. Only on ABC were Americans portrayed as more powerful than institutions; they were portrayed as the most powerful actors in 53.8 percent of that network's reports while institutions were the powerful actors an additional 30.8 percent of the time.

The big losers, obviously, were the Indians themselves, who were portrayed as powerful actors in an average of 22.9 percent of the network reports. Again there were percentage differences among the networks that were not reflected in tests for statistical significance. NBC portrayed Indians as powerful actors in 36.4 percent of its reports, but that view was reflected by CBS in only 18.2 percent of its reports and in only 15.4 percent of the stories broadcast on ABC.

The prestige press presented an even more emphatic view. Institutions were portrayed as powerful actors in more than half the prestige press stories: 56.5 percent of those printed in the *Times* and 56 percent of what ran in the *Post*. However, Indians were portrayed as powerful actors in 29.3 percent of the *Times*'s reports while Americans were powerful actors only 14.3 percent of the time. Americans were portrayed as powerful actors in 24 percent of what the *Post* printed while Indians were portrayed as powerful actors in 20 percent of the stories. These variations, again, did not reach levels of statistical significance, but the pattern of reliance on institutions as powerful actors was consistent in both publications.

The wires also maintained the institutional emphasis, although not nearly to the degree reflected in television news coverage and in reports in the prestige press. Moreover, there were statistically significant differences among the wire services.

Institutions were portrayed as the most powerful actor in Bhopal stories in 38.3 percent of all wire service reports, 39.7 percent of what ran on AP, 45.1 percent of what ran on UPI but in only

27.7 percent of the Reuters's stories. Reuters, instead, portrayed Americans as the most powerful actors in 37 percent of its stories, followed closely by Indians, 35.3 percent. It was the only media outlet studied to place institutions and those representing them in "third" place as powerful actors in the event.

Both the AP and UPI portrayed Indians as the second most powerful figures in the Bhopal story. AP portrayed Indians as the most powerful actors in 33.9 percent of what it ran while UPI portrayed Indians in the same fashion in 29.2 percent of its stories. Indians were portrayed as powerful actors in 32.7 percent of all wire service reports.

Americans were not viewed as powerful actors as frequently as Indians by the two American wire services. While Americans were portrayed as powerful actors in 29.0 percent of all wire service coverage, AP portrayed Americans as powerful in only 26.5 percent of what it wrote while UPI's stories portrayed Americans as powerful actors somewhat less frequently, 25.7 percent of the time.

Thus the wire services, in terms of powerful actors in the Bhopal story, spread the influence more evenly. It is perhaps a little ironic, or perhaps historical commentary, that the British news service was the only media outlet studied that viewed Americans as the most powerful actors in an Indian tragedy. It was certainly not a view the American media shared, for domestic news reports located the center of power firmly in institutions that, at least in the case of corporate entities such as Union Carbide, crossed national boundaries.

The newsmagazines provided the only genuine counterpoint to this view of the powerful actors in the Bhopal tragedy. But the harmonies were subtle. In the newsmagazines, Americans were portrayed as the most powerful actors in the Bhopal tragedy 44.8 percent of the time—and in 56.3 percent of the *Time* reports and 50 percent of what was printed in *U.S. News*. Only *Newsweek* deviated—the magazine portrayed Americans as the most powerful actors in only 14.3 percent of what it published.

The letters to the editor printed in *Time*, many of which held Americans responsible for the event, probably distorted the statistical analysis of the magazine's portrayal. In any case, institutions were the second most powerful actors in 34.5 percent of the magazine reports—31.3 percent in *Time*, 42.9 percent in *Newsweek* and 33.3 percent in *U.S. News*. Indians generally were not portrayed as powerful actors. Only 20.7 percent of the magazine stories portrayed Indians as the most powerful actors in the event, 12.5 percent of what was printed in *Time* and 16.7 percent of the *U.S. News* reports.

However, *Newsweek,* perhaps because its coverage was so victim-oriented, allotted Indians significant roles as powerful actors in what it printed. Fully 42.9 percent of the magazine's reports included portrayals of Indians as the most powerful actors in the Bhopal tragedy—an allotment which equaled the power status accorded to institutions in the magazine's reports.

Portraits of power were one side of the Bhopal disaster. The other side was helplessness, a tone which, it could be argued, belonged in a story about 2,000 or more people dying from an accidental gas leak. Such a tone of helplessness, it also has been argued, is a condition of news—most of which is bad and the bulk of which can be considered injurious to individuals or particular groups. Nonetheless, as a mitigation strategy, helplessness is probably not the best coping method and does not lend itself to actions which could be considered either preventive or predictive. But feelings of helplessness were an underlying tone in much of the media coverage of Bhopal. The impact of those feelings has some significant consequences for the larger meaning of the Bhopal story, both as interpreted by individuals and as assimilated in a culture which assigns meaning to events.

HELPLESSNESS

Helplessness is a fact of life—at least a fact of life as recorded in the news. Whether it is a report of a crime, a pending change in Social Security regulations or a natural or technological disaster, individuals are seldom portrayed as powerful. In fact, studies of helplessness in the news indicate that most news reports score somewhere in the mild to moderate range of thematic helplessness, defined as the ability of actors to alter events significantly (Levine, 1977).

Such was the case with Bhopal, although the visual content of television news scored somewhat higher on the helplessness scale than did the words without the pictures. But the mass media were consistent in their inclusion of thematic helplessness as part of the events in Bhopal, albeit with some statistical variation.

The *Washington Post* and the *New York Times* reports, as a collective, scored from mild to severe on the helplessness scale. While 36.8 percent of what appeared in the prestige press was judged not to have an underlying tone of helplessness, 26.9 percent of what was printed carried a mild tone of helplessness, 14.8 percent a strong helplessness tone, 11.2 percent a severe tone of helplessness and 10.3 percent a tone of extreme helplessness. Thus about 63 percent of the stories that appeared in the prestige press included an underlying tone of helplessness.

However, there was a significant difference between the two publications (Chi square = .0076). The *Times*, which included more scientific stories as well as more stories about the immediate events in Bhopal, generally scored somewhat higher on the helplessness scale. In fact, 13.9 percent of what the *Times* printed was judged to reflect a severe tone of helplessness; only one of the *Post*'s stories fit into this category. The *Post*, because it played the story from a political angle, where at least the appearance of efficacy is crucial, scored lower on the scale.

The newsmagazines, with their more issue-oriented content, reflected the general trend established in the prestige press, and there was no statistically significant difference among them. About 40 percent of the stories appearing in the three newsmagazines did not include an underlying tone of helplessness. However, 20 percent of the magazine stories ranked moderate on the helplessness scale and an additional 17.8 percent ranked in the severe range. Only 6.7 percent of the magazine stories were considered in the extreme range on the helplessness scale while 15.6 percent of what the magazines printed scored "mild" on the scale. Thus, almost half of what the newsmagazines published did not include thematic tones of helplessness, and those stories which did include such a tone tended to portray weaker elements of helplessness than did similar coverage in the prestige press.

The wires with their largely event-oriented coverage provided some variation, for only 28.9 percent of the wire service copy was judged not to include thematic helplessness content. About one-third, 33.5 percent, of the wire service reports were ranked as mild on the helplessness scale, and an additional 22.8 percent were scored as moderate. However, only 11.98 percent of the wire reports ranked as strong on the helplessness scale and even fewer stories, 3.1 percent, were judged in the extreme helplessness category.

However, like the prestige press, there were significant differences among the wire reports (Chi square = .0456). The bulk of AP's coverage, 61.7 percent, ranked mild or moderate on the helplessness scale. UPI reports followed almost exactly the same trend: 57.7 percent of its stories fell in the mild to moderate range. Reuters coverage, on the other hand, was shaded even lower on the scale. About 41 percent of its reports were judged not to contain underlying themes of helplessness, and an additional 26.5 percent of Reuters stories ranked only in the mild range.

Interpretation of such a trend is difficult. However, because Reuters covered the story from a primarily Indian angle, while the two American wire services connected events much more closely to this country, it is possible that the legal wrangling over the leak and the various problems in Institute could have shaded American reports more toward a feeling of helplessness. However, it is important to note that a majority of stories on all three wires included some thematic depiction of helplessness. Whether such reportage is an accurate reflection of the Bhopal reality, or a manifestation of traditional definitions of news, or some combination of the two, is more open to debate.

Television was different. As a whole, television coverage conveyed the impression of mild to severe helplessness 80.5 percent of the time. Only 12.2 of the television scripts—analyzed without reference to the video—were judged as not containing themes of helplessness. When the "kickers" (the last line of a television news story which is, by tradition, the second strongest line of the piece) were analyzed separately, the impression of helplessness shifted from mild-to-moderate to moderate-to-severe. These findings are, of course, influenced by television's focus on the immediate events of Bhopal rather than longer-range policy questions.

The overall media portrait of power is troubling: people as victims rather than sources of information, institutions as the powerful actors in the event, not only in terms of possessing information but also in terms of their ability to influence events, and a dominance of underlying themes of helplessness. Such portraits, at least on a cultural level, take on the aura of myth in an attempt to provide meaning for the event. The Bhopal coverage provides an example of a new cultural myth in the making. It is a myth of mass extinction, reinforced by metaphor as well as by the more obvious meaning of the events. And the myth does not bode well for the policy decisions which the increasing presence of technological hazards will require in democratic societies.

THE EMERGENCE OF A NEW CULTURAL MYTH

News is part of a cultural process which imparts meaning to various forms of knowledge. As narrative, news is orienting (Park, 1940), contextual (Belman, 1977; Smith, 1979) and ritualistic (Carey, 1975). Individual news stories themselves are not generally considered myth, but the process of gathering and distributing information about particular events or a series of events is analogous to the role of folklore or myth in contemporary culture. Malinowski (1974) considers myth to be a charter for human culture, enabling members of a culture to learn values and define right and wrong. Myth can also reassure by providing contextual meaning for certain frightening phenomena and by providing acceptable answers. Myth does not necessarily reflect an objective reality, and some scholars have noted that cultural "troubles" arise when the myth structures underlying society diverge from reality so significantly that the society itself is prevented from experimenting with needed changes.

Myth also generally involves the retelling of "age old" stories with modern interpretations. But, occasionally, the culture, in response to stresses and developments within, creates a new myth or radically alters an existing myth to imbue it with new or more functional meanings. Media reportage of Bhopal provides the latest example of modern, Western culture's attempt to give meaning to society's knowledge of its technological ability to create widespread death and destruction, including possible societal and biological extinction. In this sense, news coverage of Bhopal is important for not only what it says, but also for how various facts are interpreted within a cultural frame.

Ancient Western culture has little myth structure surrounding the notion of societal extinction, and most of what exists is Biblical. The Judeo-Christian tradition provides several accounts of widespread extinction: the tale of Sodom and Gomorrah, the deaths of Egypt's first-born, the Great Flood, and perhaps the drowning of the Egyptian armies in the Red Sea. The New Testament's Book of Revelation is widely interpreted as a mythical recounting of the end of the world, specific debates as to its literal accuracy notwithstanding. The Middle Ages provide another example of mass extinction: the deaths caused by plague which, in the ensuing centuries, have taken on a somewhat mythical cast.

These basic myths have several common elements. They attribute extinction to forces beyond humanity's control, in the Biblical instances to a wrathful God and in the Middle Ages to a bacterium no one knew existed and a lack of antibiotics. In this sense, mass destruction was visted on the offending society from above, and people could do little either to explain the destruction or defend against it. Individual helplessness is also a primary component of such myth structures, as is the role of institutional religion, in the Biblical case, and lack of institutional preparedness, in the case of the Middle Ages.

The invention and use of poison gas as a weapon in the twentieth century has begun to alter fundamentally this existing mythical view. German and Allied use of phosgene (mustard gas) in World War I changed the myth in significant ways. First, the poison itself was the result of modern science, unlike God's wrath or the plague bacterium. Second, the decision to use the gas was made by human beings, not by God or by some other invisible agency. Thus the existence of the death–causing agent itself and the decision to use it became human-centered in a way that Biblical accounts or interpretations of the plague would not allow. In addition, it is important to note that phosgene is a component of the modern pesticide MIC, which was responsible for the deaths and injuries in Bhopal.

World War I's most famous gas victim, of course, was Adolph

Hitler. The Fuhrer added new layers of meaning to extinction myths, specifically his notions of racial superiority and the use of gas in the concentration camps. Hitler's most horrific addition to the concept is probably that such an act could be carried out as official government policy, and that those subject to that policy, with certain important and well-documented exceptions, appeared to be willing to "let it happen."

Finally, the notion of airborne poisons has become part of the vocabulary of the post-World War II era. In the United States, criminals have been executed in "gas chambers," and both the United States—in Vietnam—and the Soviet Union—in Afghanistan—have been accused of using various sorts of airborne poisons as part of their military efforts.

Thus, what began as a myth centering on the wrath of God over willful disobedience has been transformed into a myth which focuses on various products of modern society used as a deliberate part of national policy.

Bhopal's contribution to this mythical development may well be the addition of the notion of the "unintended accident which results from intentional national economic or political policies."

In this sense, the role that the poisonous substance—in the case of Bhopal, MIC—plays is a cousin of what Machiavelli referred to as "fortuna." The Indian government, for good reasons, set a national policy of "feeding itself" and gaining economic self–sufficiency early in the nation's drive for independence. Pesticides could help with both goals, providing not only a means of higher food production but also jobs. Certainly, no one intended any accidental poisoning, and certainly not a poisoning on the scale of Bhopal. But, as scientists and engineers have understood for decades, such accidents, either in the form of incomplete knowledge at the time the particular product is developed or in the form of a technology which literally "wears out" before use ceases, can and will happen. Such a context provokes the notion of unintended accident resulting from well–articulated goals. Institutions assume a dominant role. They not only possess policy and scientific information, but they are the crucial entities whose actions count. In some genuine sense, the meaning of the event—in this case the Bhopal disaster—is couched firmly within an institutional frame.

The individual citizen who becomes caught up in all these

calculations between national economic self–sufficiency and development, on the one hand, and personal safety and health, on the other, may be viewed as subject to forces outside individual control. Such loss of control leaves decisions about which technologies to employ, for what purposes, in the hands of institutions within society which may have conflicting goals or which may press for progress at extraordinarily high human costs. For such a view to take hold, the costs of technology must be economic—loss of life must be "accidental." For such a view to sustain itself, reports of such accidents need to include a sense of individual helplessness reflected not only in terms of specific acts but in many more subtle senses: for example, who is considered a "legitimate" source of information.

Certainly the news reports of Bhopal would seem to support the latest development in the evolution of a myth of societal extinction. Visual images focused on victims and on gas. The powerful figures were institutions rather than individuals. Issues of legal liability rather than long-range health and safety questions were the focus on much of the long-range debate. A majority of stories printed and broadcast scored between moderate and severe on the helplessness scale. Such issues as alternative technologies or the general problems of technological hazards were the focus of a minority of stories. Instead, what readers and viewers saw was the accidental event, the pain and suffering it caused and a number of facts about the Bhopal plant and what happened there—all placed within a framework of institutional power and thematic helplessness where short-term events dominated long-term concerns. Such reportage is truly knowledge verging on myth, for it omits both cultural and long-term contexts.

Bhopal represents an example of the next step in the evolution of a cultural myth of mass extinction. It has now become a myth where a wrathful God is replaced by human beings making policy decisions for economic or political ends. Bhopal becomes an accident, one in which institutions have a large role to play, but which simultaneously renders individuals impotent. The effects linger, but what is lacking is any attempt to frame national policy questions around the broader issue of technological hazards. It is a myth which is profoundly undemocratic for it removes citizens from those questions which have an immense capacity to influence their lives and the lives of their children. More significantly, it fails to inform citizens that they, as individuals, do have policy choices to make. It is a myth which needs creative reinterpretation, a reinterpretation which the news media, considering already documented biases, are unlikely to provide.

6

The Public Perception

Interviewer: What do you associate with the word Bhopal? That's spelled B–H–O–P–A–L.

Respondent: A car made in Japan.

Respondent: I thought of using Raid and how it makes insects die.

Respondent: Union Carbide—white, industrial, imperialism.

Perhaps the single most researched question in all media scholarship centers on what it is that people remember from the mass media and how those memories provoke or fail to provoke action. While scholars agree on the importance of the question, the variety and singular lack of concrete answers to it are perhaps the most frustrating aspects of media research. When asked—and people have been asked repeatedly—about what they recall from news media reports, responses have varied from the humorous and irrelevant to the highly abstract. Most people, most of the time, on most issues, are someplace in between.

So it was with the public memory of Bhopal. People in two communities—Eugene, Oregon, which considers itself an environmentally aware city in an environmentally conscious state, and Charleston, West Virginia, home of the sister Bhopal plant—were asked in July 1985 what they remembered about media coverage of the tragedy, almost seven months after the event. While the issue had temporarily faded from the news agenda at the time of the poll, many people maintained vivid memories of the tragedy. The fact that those memories persisted, months after the initial event, is perhaps the single most important finding of this study. Academic researchers may not know quite why it is that people remember precisely what they do, but there is little doubt that they do remember. What follows is an overview of those memories and perceptions, supported at times by individual comments. Some theoretical ruminations about why these memories may or may not make sense in a larger societal context conclude the chapter.

MEDIA USE PATTERNS

The media preference patterns for those surveyed generally reflected national trends, although newspaper readership was particularly strong. Of those surveyed, 40.3 percent cited newspapers first when asked where they obtained information about the world around them. Newspapers were the second choice for 30.1 percent of the sample, while television ranked first with 39.5 percent of those surveyed and was listed second by 36.0 percent of the respondents. Magazines and radio finished a distant third: 10.9 percent listed radio as a first choice for information about the world around them, and magazines were cited as the first choice by 10.1 percent of those surveyed.

Those responding also identified themselves as media consumers. About 52.8 percent of those sampled said they had watched the network news "last night," and 60.9 percent of the respondents indicated they had watched the network news at least four times in the past week. The figures were even higher for newspapers: 76.4 percent of those surveyed said they had read the newspaper yesterday, and 66.8 percent said they had read the newspaper at least four times during the past week with 45.1 percent saying they had read a newspaper seven times in the last seven days. A total of 66.5 percent said the household in which they lived subscribed to either the Eugene paper or one of the two Charleston newspapers. Magazine readership was much lower, with 46 percent of those surveyed saying they had not read one of the major newsmagazines in the past month, and only 16 percent noting they had read one of the three major newsmagazines at least four times in the past month.

FACTUAL RECALL

When respondents were asked what medium had provided them with most of their information about Bhopal, their responses reflected more generalized national trends. Television was the primary source of information, cited by 54.5 percent of the sample, with newspapers cited by 26.4 percent. Radio was ranked the third most informative medium, but only 7.3 percent of those sampled said they had obtained the bulk of their information about Bhopal from radio. Magazines were cited by 4.2 percent of those sampled, and talking with others was listed by 3.2 percent.

Such media consumption patterns should have resulted in some retention of factual information about the event, although a number of studies have suggested that heavy television viewing is not conducive to factual recall. However, both Charleston and Eugene residents appear to have learned and retained at least some information about the events of Bhopal six months after the disaster faded from the national news agenda.

Respondents were first asked what they "associated" with the word Bhopal. The most prominent association was "India," which was mentioned by 16.3 percent of those surveyed, although 32.4 percent of those sampled could not supply at least one factually correct association with the word. The chemical firm Union Carbide was mentioned by 7.1 percent of those who said they associated something with the word. While Union Carbide and India were the two most frequently cited "single idea" responses, many of those responding associated a number of ideas with the word. Five percent of those who answered the question responded with the concepts of "chemicals, death in India," and an additional 3.4 percent responded with the ideas of "chemicals and death" without the geographic tag. Three percent of those responding associated the word with "Union Carbide and death." Only .10 percent of those responding associated the word with local events, and .03 percent associated the term with media coverage of the event itself.

When probed about their associations with the word Bhopal, 74 percent of the sample could supply no additional details. Of those who did supply additional responses, the most common were "chemicals," mentioned by 5.4 percent of the total sample, India, mentioned by 4.7 percent of the sample, and Union Carbide, mentioned by 3.0 percent.

Factual recall extended beyond geographic identification and a vague notion of the event itself. Two-fifths of those surveyed could place the "sister" Bhopal plant in its proper geographic location. About 31.5 percent said the plant was in "Institute," 7.3 percent located it in South Charleston and an additional 2.8 percent said the plant was somewhere near Charleston but could not name the precise city. Since Insitute is an unincorporated community, some confusion about its location could be expected, even among those familiar with the area. An additional 21.7 percent of those sampled said they knew the plant was in the United States, but could not be more specific about its location, while 20.4 percent of those sampled said they did not know where the plant was located. The remainder of those sampled gave widely scattered geographic responses, the most common of which were "Africa" and "some place in South America."

People also recalled some specific facts about the impact of the event. About 35.6 percent of those responding gave the "correct" answer—between 2,000 and 2,500—when asked how many people had died as a result of the leak. A total of 25 percent of those responding said fewer than 2,500 had died in the accident, although specific figures varied widely. About 25.2 percent of those responding said they did not know how many had died.

However, people did not retain as much information about the number of injured. More than half the sample, 53.6 percent, said they did not know how many people were injured, and only 4.3 percent were able to respond with the correct answer— 200,000 to 250,000. Of the total sample, 39.9 percent responded with 100,000 people or less. Clearly, the number of injured was not as vivid or as accurate in the public memory as was the number of the dead.

People also knew who owned the Indian plant. About 64.1

percent of those surveyed correctly responded that the plant belonged to Union Carbide, and only 27.3 percent said they did not know the owner. The remainder of those responding split among the other major U.S. chemical firms, Dow and Monsanto.

The long-term health and environmental impact of the event also was vividly etched in the minds of those who responded. The vast majority of those sampled said they believed the accident would cause permanent lung damage (89.6 percent) and eye problems (86.0 percent). In contrast, those sampled were relatively sure the chemical spill would not cause arthritis (51 percent), with an additional 35.7 percent saying they did not know if the spill would result in that particular disability. Responses were similar for heart attacks: 59.4 percent said the spill would not cause heart attacks, and an additional 21.4 percent said they did not know. (Several respondents, however, noted that people probably had heart attacks during the event, but not caused by the gas itself.)

The only anomaly in factual recall appeared when respondents were asked if they believed the MIC spill would cause cancer, something that was not mentioned frequently in news reports and which is an issue on which science is not definitive. Despite these "facts," 71.9 percent of those surveyed said they believed the spill would cause cancer, and only 17.8 percent were uncertain about the relationship between exposure and the disease.

Two other sections of the survey attempted to probe feelings of helplessness, or vulnerability, to the sort of event Bhopal represented. Respondents were asked to select one of two choices in four statements about different aspects of the event, ranging from an individual's ability to protect self and family in the event of a chemical leak to the notion that chemical spills may harm future generations, a psychological response which has been documented by Lifton (1967), in his work on the survivors of Hiroshima. In that series of questions, 76.7 percent of those surveyed selected the statement "we should be able to prevent accidents like the one in Bhopal"; 48.7 percent said that, should such an accident occur, they would be able "to do some things to protect" themselves and their families; 56.4 percent said increased government regulation would result in a decrease in such accidents; while 73.2 percent of the respondents said they believe accidents like the one in Bhopal would harm future generations.

The feelings these questions aroused, particularly in Charleston residents, were readily apparent. One resident told the interviewer, "It's a crime to locate chemical plants . . . in residential areas . . . we aren't told about potential hazards and this angers me. We are taught to depend on experts and wonder how much we are really told. . . . We have chemical plants here and wonder what potential hazards there are . . . after the Bhopal tragedy."

Some also connected the questions to events in their own lives. One man responded, "Before the accident I had heard nothing about it. Up until that happened, I didn't know the chemicals they made in my backyard were so deadly. I just knew they made pesticides." Another commented, "I used to work for Allied Chemicals. I have chemical burns on both legs. . . . I know what it does when you sweat and it activates it and leaves terrible scars. The gasses mess up your lungs and skin and can make lungs collapse. I've had nine years experience. . . . "

In a similar vein, 25.5 percent of those surveyed said they or family members had been personally involved in a chemical spill or some other form of technological hazard, 59.4 percent of those surveyed said they lived in a town or a city where such an event had occurred, and 21 percent said they had had some personal experience with a natural hazard, such as a flood or earthquake, in the past five years.

Finally, people said they remembered what they had seen and read about the event. The most memorable medium was television, with only 31.9 percent of those surveyed saying they did not remember any of the television coverage of the event. The most memorable element of television coverage was the visual image—specifically the visual images of death on the screen. Thus, 7.8 percent of those responding said the television pictures were the most memorable elements of the coverage without referring to specific images, and an additional 11.1 percent said the images of death were the most memorable to them. An additional 7.1 percent of those surveyed said they remembered both the overall images of Bhopal and connected those to specific pictures of the dead and the dying. Twelve percent said they retained a general impression of "tragedy" without any recall of specific pictures.

For example, one respondent remembered "people who were destroyed . . . a little girl who was killed and being buried." Another said he recalled "large numbers of people running from the explosion and breathing in more of the gas than if they had stayed put . . . also, how close people lived to the plant."

An Institute resident noted that television had summoned other images to her mind. "It was like a nuclear war had happened. Shocking . . . frightening. They then revealed they were making MIC here. It was terrifying to see the suffering people" A 30-year-old man, who worked for the West Virginia state government, recalled the television pictures of "human suffering, personal anguish . . . government officials were very angry."

Specific elements in the events of Bhopal, for example, Union Carbide Chairman Warren Anderson's Indian visit, were cited by only a very few as memorable portions of television coverage. However, 3.0 percent of those surveyed recalled images of people helping each other and an additional 2.3 percent said they recalled the television coverage focusing on a "lack of preparation" by Union Carbide and the Indian people for such an event. Finally, about 5.3 percent of those surveyed were able to provide multidetailed responses, specific memories of a particular television news report or a specific image or sets of images.

But, sometimes, recall of specific television reports led to the creation of other sorts of memorable images. One Eugene respondent said television reports of the lawyers arriving in Bhopal reminded him of "flies on a dead cow."

The public memory of newspaper coverage of the event differed in crucial ways. First, the newspaper reports generally were not recalled as vividly: 47.7 percent of those responding said they could remember nothing about the newspaper reports of the event. For those who did recall specific stories or impressions, the overriding pattern was again a recall of images of death with an increase in the number of specific events people were able to recall. Thus, only 1.5 percent of those polled said they recalled pictures of Bhopal printed in newspapers, while 8.3 percent said they recalled the "deaths" associated with the event and an identical percentage said they retained an overall impression of "tragedy."

However, 4.9 percent of those surveyed said their most vivid recollection of newspaper coverage was stories about who was to blame for the Bhopal disaster, and an additional 5.9 percent said they recalled stories focusing on the local impact of the event and local safety regulations and preparedness issues.

"They blamed Union Carbide," one man said of his recall of newspaper reports. "But India owned 49 percent and they weren't blamed." Others, too, recalled discussions of responsibility and blame in the print media. One respondent said what she most remembered were stories about why "safety issues were ignored."

Still others said they were impressed by the lack of bias in newspaper reports. "I was impressed that coverage was unbiased, and they presented both sides." Such a view, however, was not universal. A 45-year-old unemployed man responded, "All accounts in newspapers are only 55 percent true . . . they're not an accurate report and they tell you only what they want you to know. They get the rest from unreliable sources." The same man said he believed television was the far more accurate medium.

Newspaper stories about the flocking of lawyers to Bhopal were recalled by 2.4 percent of those surveyed and 1.3 percent recalled stories about Anderson's visit. The newspaper coverage of the event itself, without any specific reference to particular stories or issues, was cited as memorable by 3.2 percent of those surveyed. Finally, about 3.2 percent of those surveyed provided "multidetailed" portraits of specific stories or accounts they found most memorable, although the subject matter of those reports varied widely.

Magazine coverage was the least memorable to those sampled, hardly surprising since magazine readership was far below television viewing or newspaper readership. About 78.1 percent of those sampled could recall nothing about magazine coverage, and those memories that did exist were scattered among a variety of topics. However, among those topics pictures were again among the most memorable items, recalled by 1.6 percent of all those surveyed and including pictures of the dead and the dying.

"Time gave an accurate account of the whole issue . . . it showed pictures of the people crippled." Another respondent accurately recalled a magazine photo "with the person being led while carrying a child." Others, however, merely said the magazines they read provided more depth.

Magazine readers, too, retained a general impression of the tragedy—3.9 percent of those surveyed—and of the number of dead—1.4 percent. About 2.0 percent of those surveyed said the magazine stories most memorable to them were stories about the media coverage of the event.

THE INFLUENCE OF THE ENVIRONMENT

If the uses and gratifications approach is correct, particularly with regard to human needs for security, then the environment—and the relative security of that environment—should have an impact not only on what people bring "to the media they use" but also what they take away from them. Tests for differences in the way Eugene and Charleston residents responded to the survey tended to support this view.

First, there were no statistically significant differences in the way residents of the two communities said they used the media to learn what was going on in the world around them, or about Bhopal itself. In addition, there was no significant difference in the number of "heavy television viewers, those who said they watched the national network news at least four times in the past week" in the two communities. Charleston residents were significantly more likely (Chi square = .0026) to have read a newspaper at least four times in the past week. There was no statistically significant difference in magazine readership.

Despite generally similar patterns of media use, Charleston residents were significantly more in command of the "facts" of Bhopal. Charleston residents were significantly more likely to cite the correct death toll as a result of the Bhopal disaster than were Eugene residents, and Charleston residents also were significantly more likely to give the correct location of the "sister" Bhopal plant.

There was no significant difference between Eugene residents and Charleston residents in their ability to correctly recall the number of injured. In fact, more than half those surveyed, 196 in Charleston and 223 in Eugene, responded "don't know" to the question.

Charleston residents also were much more likely to correctly name the corporate owner of the Bhopal plant. However, Charleston residents were not significantly more likely than Eugene residents to say that media reports "blamed" any person or group for the disaster, nor were Charleston residents who said the media did "blame someone or something" more likely to name a specific group or corporation as "blamed by the media".

Increased knowledge of the events in Bhopal by Charleston residents did not—with two possible exceptions—carry over into the long-term health effects issues. There was no significant difference between Eugene and Charleston residents on whether the leak would cause heart attacks, arthritis, or permanent lung damage. However, significantly more Eugene residents responded that the leak would cause eye problems and cancer.

These responses on the health questions are noteworthy for two reasons. First, initial media reports, particularly television reports, indicated many people were "blinded" by the MIC leak. In fact, no one was permanently blinded, although about 20 percent of those exposed to the gas are, at current estimates, expected to have some permanent vision loss.

Second, while a larger percentage of the total sample said the leak would cause cancer, fewer Charleston residents expressed this belief. The scientific debate on whether high concentrations of MIC could act as a carcinogen has yet to be resolved. In addition, the death rate as a result of lung and other forms of respiratory cancer in the valley in which Charleston is located is 21 percent over the national norm. Thus, on one level, the responses of the Charleston residents to these two health questions could be considered "more knowledgeable" than those of people living in Eugene. Whether that knowledge came from the mass media, particularly print reports which carried much more detail about the health effects, or is the result of detailed attention to the event, repression or some other process remains an open question.

Residents of the two communities also provided significantly different responses on two of the "helplessness" questions included in the survey. There was no significant difference between Eugene and Charleston residents in their response to the generalized issue of whether "accidents like the one in Bhopal are bound to happen" and the more specific question of whether increased government regulation would decrease the chances of Bhopal-like disasters. However, the two communities did diverge on the issue of whether "there are things I could do to protect myself and my family" in the event of a chemical spill. On that question, significantly more Charleston residents felt they could help themselves and their families. On the issue of whether disasters like the one in Bhopal harm not only this but future generations, Eugene residents were significantly more pessimistic.

While it is impossible to say definitely that the realities of life in an environment with eleven separate chemical plants makes a difference in what people recall about salient events, several other findings are worth some note. There was no significant difference between the two communities in age, occupation, level of schooling, income or sex. However, there was a marked difference between the two communities in personal or community involvement with technological hazards. Charleston residents were significantly more likely to have been personally involved with a technological hazard or to have a family member involved with a technological hazard. Charleston residents were significantly more likely to say they lived in a town or city where such events took place. On one level, these findings represent only common sense. On a second level, they may reflect the salience of such events to residents of the two communities; they provide some indication to the "needs" for surveillance or security residents may bring to their reading and viewing of news reports.

THE IMPACT OF PERSONAL EXPERIENCE ON MEDIA USE

When the respondents were divided into two groups, those who both read the newspaper at least four times a week and watched network television news at least four times a week, and those who did not, another pattern emerged. Heavy media users were significantly more likely to have been personally involved, or to have a family member involved, with a technological hazard, or to live in a community which had been the site of a technological hazard. This relationship, however, did not carry over into involvement with a natural hazard.

Again, interpretation of these findings requires caution. While the results do not suggest a causal relationship, they may point toward some generalized notion of individual needs for environmental surveillance based on past personal experience. One method for establishing such an individual "environmental watch" may be some increased media use.

FEELINGS OF HELPLESSNESS AND IMAGE RECALL

Some media scholars also have suggested a relationship between media reportage of events—primarily political events—and individual feelings of unease about the political process or political actors. Other scholars have suggested such long-term effects may permeate other fields, hence the recent investigations of the impact of "bad news." While the findings from the public opinion survey generally did not support such conclusions, there was one important exception. People who tended to categorize events such as the one in Bhopal as "bound to happen," or to believe that events in Bhopal harmed not only those now living but also future generations, carried different pictures in their heads of the Bhopal tragedy months after it happened.

Specifically, those who said they believed accidents like this one in Bhopal were bound to happen were significantly more likely to recall the images of death in television coverage of the event and less likely to recall images of medical problems, cooperation or stories focusing on local aspects of the event. Such relationships, however, did not persist in recall of newspaper or magazine stories.

The trend was even more pronounced among those people who said they believed accidents like the one in Bhopal would harm future generations. Images of death dominated the memories of those agreed with that statement, while local stories and discrete events were more memorable to those who said they believed the consequences of such an accident would be restricted to this generation.

Again, such results must be interpreted with caution. Lifton, in his work on the Japanese victims of the atomic bomb, has noted one of the most striking responses he observed was the psychological image that the bomb would end not only this life but *all* life, both plant and animal, now and forever. It may well be that some of this feeling of the end of all life pervades individual views of technological hazard. Such a predisposition, of course, is not without some basis in fact; science is aware of the mutagenic qualities of both radioactivity and some chemicals. That such an individual predisposition could be reinforced by memories of death in the television coverage of a Bhopal-like event would be the standard interpretation by many media scholars. Why such a relationship would not carry over into all areas of helplessness—for example, the efficacy of increased government regulation—and why such a relationship would manifest itself only for television reportage, remain important, unanswered questions.

A PRELIMINARY THEORETICAL FRAME

Bhopal is in many ways a symptom rather than a disease. While the incident is, at one level, the largest industrial accident in human history, it is also, on another level, an accident waiting to happen in other countries in other industries. News reports of such events, and the deeper issues which those events raise, as well as public memory of that coverage, may provide mass media scholars with some important insights to the "hows and whys" of individual media use.

In that vein, I would like to suggest media scholars adopt a view of the uses and gratifications approach which, with some success, has been used in fields such as political science. That approach, simplified, may be summarized as $B = f(O) E$, or behavior is the function of an organism—in this case a particular human being—within an environment (Davies, 1963). Media scholars might adapt the concept as follows: $MUM = f(O)E$ or

Media *Use* and *Memory* is a function of an individual organism, with certain needs, in a particular environment.

Such a conceptualization helps to explain the public memory of Bhopal. Media use would reflect a generalized need for environmental surveillance, regardless of specific geographic location. However, certain environments—for example, life in a valley with eleven different chemical plants—may demand both a different level of surveillance through the mass media and a different level of factual information retention. To be sure, the mass media would be one of many surveillance methods employed, but for events such as the one in Bhopal, the media would be among the most important. Given that most individuals have a need to remain alive—an issue on which there is little debate even among the various schools of psychology—then individuals in a "more hazardous" environment could be expected to meet that need, in part, through heavier media use and through greater retention of information and images presented by the mass media. Such a conceptualization would explain why Charleston residents were more factually accurate about the events of Bhopal than were residents of "environmentally conscious" Eugene.

However, such an explanation takes into account only the relationship between survival, a particular environment and a generalized notion of mass media use. Human organisms have needs other than mere survival. Foremost among them is the need for power in the sense of the ability to influence the physical and psychological environment. Put in simpler terms, this need for power is the reason babies cry; they wail to summon parents who, in turn, teach them that even as tiny individuals they have some rudimentary ability to control their environments. Such a sense of control has been accepted as one of the building blocks of self-esteem. Lack of control, or the perception of control, has, in its turn, been linked with depression, apathy and loss of ego strength.

Hazards scholars also have noted that a sense of efficacy, the perceived role of individual and government, may be highly influential (Burton, Kates and White, 1978). Scholars have found that a major component of individual response to hazards is a sense of responsibility the individual possesses about the situation and possible methods to remedy it. "According to this view, what the individual does is strongly related to his recognition of his capacity to act and his sense of social responsibility to do so" (Burton et al. 1978: 107).

It may be that, in relatively healthy adults, this need for a perception of control may vary in time, place and in relation to certain issues. One way people may seek to confirm their own internalized notions may be through the mass media. The mass media, in its turn, may reinforce, subtly shift or amplify those already preexisting cognitive structures. People who believe themselves to be helpless about certain events, such as chemical spills, may take away from media coverage of those spills images which simultaneously reinforce a preexisting belief while amplifying those aspects of it which most closely conform to individual perceptions. Visual images may add to the potency of the process. This psychological need for control of the environment may be enhanced or diminished by a synergistic interaction between human needs and the mass media, all of which exist within a particular environment.

Thus, those who believe themselves to be helpless in the area of technological hazards may retain images of the dead and the dying contained within media reports, perhaps to the exclusion of more positive images. The environment in which an individual lives, and past personal or community experience with such an event may, in turn, amplify or in other ways alter that process. Such a schema may help media scholars explain why people remember what they remember—at least when needs for security are highly salient. Such a schema also may provide hazards scholars with some important insights into public perceptions of technological events.

7

What Price Connection?

BHOPAL'S MEDIATED REALITY

On December 4, 1984, Dan Rather began the CBS evening news with a somber recounting of the mounting death toll after a chemical leak in Bhopal, India: by official estimate more than 1,000 dead, the majority of them children. The video portion of the five-minute report, the first actual footage of the December 3 disaster aired on CBS, opened with scenes of rows of unidentified, sheet-covered bodies lining the lawn of the overflowing Bhopal morgue. As the voice-over recounted the basic facts of what was known about the number of dead and injured, the camera focused on the dead—bodies being loaded into trucks, close–ups of the faces of unknown victims, and the mounting funeral pyres.

At the end of that segment of the report, the network aired footage of a child's burial. While the reporter noted many of Bhopal's children "were buried, not cremated, according to religious custom," the camera took about eight seconds to show an infant boy being lowered into a shallow grave. The final image on the screen was three pairs of adult hands placing the infant in the earth. While the child's face was visible to viewers, the faces of the adults burying him were not.

Similar scenes played for more than two weeks on all three networks.

Scenes of the dead, the dying and the living victims were a

focal point of the early television coverage, and, indeed, the events that produced so much death and injury were the focus of all media reports.

In one particularly vivid television report, the camera focused on an Indian doctor, giving obviously futile mouth-to-mouth resuscitation to a child. Suddenly the doctor stopped, looked up at those nearest, spread his hands in a universal gesture of futility, and shook his head. In the next scene, the obviously distraught physician was interviewed in the hall outside the ward. "Children are dying, and I can't do anything about it," he said.

The scene is important for two reasons. First, in only sixteen instances, in ten out of forty-one stories, were Indians portrayed as "powerful figures"—that is, those capable of doing something about or influencing the events in Bhopal. Americans, on the other hand, were portrayed as powerful actors thirty-nine times, in twenty of the forty-one stories. Second, the scene itself lacked context. The Bhopal medical community made massive efforts in the days and weeks after the disaster, despite a doctors' strike and a lack of information about the toxic effects of MIC. While the doctors could not save everyone, they saved many—and despite early reports, no one was blinded as a result of the chemical spill, although about 20 percent of those exposed to the gas sustained partial sight loss. This story—that is, the work of the Indian medical community in the midst of the crisis— went largely unreported. Only the *New York Times* and Reuters carried reports about the efforts; the television networks failed to mention them.

The networks also failed on a more fundamental level. They generally provided no information to warn viewers of potential similar events and the long-term coverage of the Bhopal clean-up was restricted to reports about the neutralization of the gas remaining at the plant and the impact the leak would have on Indian elections. In contrast to other media, television provided almost no information about the cultural background of India or Bhopal, and it chose to frame the economics of the story in terms of Carbide survival rather than asking questions about why the plant had been built in Bhopal, the impact of the Green Revolution and the tough choices governments make when they balance widespread starvation against the risks of importing imperfect, often enormously beneficial, technology. These issues were all a central part of the Bhopal story, and while none of the media outlets studied did a thorough job covering them, television was the only outlet studied which omitted mention of most of them entirely.

Thus the totality of television's Bhopal coverage initially raises two ethical questions. First, what is the balance between truthful, comprehensive coverage and the need for individual privacy? Second, do such events, particularly in the Third World, lead to stereotypical portraits of those involved? However, Bhopal raises deeper issues, for the event is nothing if not a symptom of a worldwide industrial disease. Humanity's shared vulnerability—regardless of geography—to such technological hazards may somehow demand a different form of reportage, one which emphasizes evaluation and analysis of the value framework underlying scientific and technological discovery.

THE HINDU WAY OF DEATH

Western reportage on an Eastern culture raises a number of sensitive issues, prominent among them the tendency of the dominant culture to inflict its mores and values on an alternate belief system. Television journalists made scant but nonetheless pointed references to cultural and religious differences between Indians and Americans, particularly in the area of religious ceremonies. While many of the ethical issues surrounding the Bhopal reportage do not directly reflect on a clash of cultures, it is important for the overall discussion of the ethical issues to have some understanding of the cultural and religious underpinnings of Indian society.[1]

For Hindus, fire is the medium of life; it is a communication link between man and the gods. This relationship is made meaningful by a series of rituals which begin before birth and continue through childhood, and which are designed to anchor the child firmly in the karma of this life. In young children, there is the sense that the child has not yet lived long enough in ritual to make purification by fire—cremation—necessary upon death.

Thus, young children, generally those below the age of one year, are buried rather than cremated.

Hindus do not view a corpse with the same strong emotional attachment generally associated with Western belief. A prominent tenet of Hinduism is that the body is insignificant compared to the soul; this belief is similar to the traditional Judeo-Christian concept. Hindus, through belief and practice, develop a fairly quick disattachment from the body; there is no lengthy mourning period.

Coexisting with this belief is the popular view that looking on or touching a corpse brings with it a negative spirit or karma. Indians who look at or touch a corpse would consider themselves polluted by the act and should be purified by later rites. The crucial tenet of this social more is, however, that the bad karma adheres to those who have engaged in the act of pollution. Indians, at least those upper–class Hindus who may have seen some of the coverage, would view the scenes of the dead not so much as an invasion of privacy but as the accrual of bad karma by Western journalists. Most of the insult of the act would be directed to those in the West who saw the pictures and who would reap bad karma from the activity.

Finally, the poor and illiterate, who were the majority of the victims of Bhopal, were probably overwhelmed by the event. The death of a child, particularly a male child, is a calamity for Hindus. But the Indian people by custom and religious tradition are inclined to share such a loss with family and friends as a coping mechanism. Such a sharing is seldom a large-scale public display of the sort that media exposure provides. The poor and the illiterate have fewer physical means of "covering" such things. In Bhopal the shock and the poverty made it easy for journalists to get vivid pictures. What is less certain is whether the Indians welcomed the attention.

THE INITIAL ISSUES

Disasters like the one in Bhopal present both print and broadcast journalists with a set of challenges. The first of them is that the number of bodies and the depth of the destruction seem to tax the powers of the English language. Before television, Jack

London in his coverage of the 1906 San Francisco earthquake, tried his hand at description of destruction on a massive scale.

> The earthquake shook down in San Francisco hundreds of thousands of dollars worth of walls and chimneys. But the conflagration that followed burned up hundreds of millions of dollars worth of property. There is no estimating within hundreds of millions the actual damage wrought. Not in history has a modern imperial city been so completely destroyed. San Francisco is gone (Snyder and Morris, 1962:269).

Bhopal provided journalists with a challenge equal to that of the San Francisco quake, and many rose to the occasion. John S. Lang, writing in the December 17 issue of *U.S. News & World Report*, painted this word portrait.[2]

> The cloud of poison gas that oozed death and agony through a sleeping city in India has awakened the world to a danger hanging over mankind.
> It's a nightmare come true—the 2,000 dead and 100,000 injured in the city of Bhopal—of what can happen anywhere that people live close to the powerful tools they try to use to master their environment.
> Bhopal became a hell. Seventy funeral pyres, stacked 25 bodies high, all burning at once. Mass graves near overflowing. Babies gasping for breath in hospitals that reported a death a minute. Streets strewn with carcasses of animals. Swarms of flies. Skies with circling vultures.
> The city of 900,000 people stank of death. The leaves on trees shriveled and yellowed. Ponds got scummy. Turnips and spinach grew scorched in the fields, milk turned foul. Everywhere sounded the wails of grieving relatives, moans of survivors in pain and cries of hungry children.

Dean Brelis, *Time*'s New Delhi Bureau Chief, wrote in the December 17 issue, "I have seen more killed in battle. But seeing ordinary people dying before your eyes, especially mute children falling dead in a transfixed silence, is appalling. I felt as if I were wandering through a landscape of the dead."[3] And Roger Rosenblat, in an essay on that same issue, noted: "Human progress came up against human frailty. The air was poisoned, and the world gasped."[4]

But television has a weapon besides words in its "truth-telling" arsenal. It is one thing to describe a child dying. It is another to show a doctor tell parents and loved ones that a child is dead, to witness the doctor's frustration over his inability to save more lives and to see an infant, unobscured by coffin or shroud, buried. Indeed, it is television's ability to "show" rather than "tell" which makes its reportage so potent.

Pictures, reporters and editors could reasonably argue, reveal a symbolic truth about Bhopal. The human connection between those pictured on the television screen and those who might someday be pictured as a result of economic and political policies that accept normal accidents is the underlying reality of technological disaster.

But this simultaneously factual and symbolic television story, when it reached American living rooms, raised some troubling questions. First, the images of death and injury were repeated many times on many evenings. The sheer volume of them raises the issue of whether the dead and dying were used to heighten viewer attentiveness—and hence ratings—rather than exclusively to convey the story. The fact that television, except through pictures, seldom chose to raise those larger issues adds some weight to the question.

Second, there was no discussion of the admittedly complicated and alien views surrounding the Hindu concept of death. Readers and viewers were left without guidance as to how to interpret culturally what they were seeing, although they were alerted there were important differences in world view. Without such backgrounding, what many probably saw was an invasion of privacy on a rather substantial and consistent basis. Americans seeing these pictures might legitimately wonder if reporters and cameras would invade their religious ceremonies or burial rites, if the gas leak had occurred in Institute rather than Bhopal. Indeed, past media practice indicates that such might be the case.[6]

Third, the overall portrait of Indians painted by the media coverage was a stereotypical one: Indians were people without power, viewed in terms of death and destruction. The effective actions of the Indian medical community were not "used" to round out the portrait. This stereotypical view of "people of color" was more subtly underlined by the televison camera's willingness to focus on private acts of grief, mourning and interment. The overall impact—which was probably unintentional—was to portray Indians as something less than competent, responsive human beings. It was coverage which by inference rather than overt statement denied the dignity of those being covered.

Christians (1983) and Hodges (1983) have noted that, in an ethical sense, to stereotype and to invade privacy denies dignity. Hodges notes:

> The mere fact that people would be interested to know is just not enough to warrant the harm done to an individual by an invasion of his or her circles of intimacy. The significant harm to the individual seems to me to outweigh the public benefit. To deny a person control over his circles of intimacy is to deny that person a measure of his dignity (Hodges, 1983:12).

Christians reinforces the point. "The dignity of persons ought not be maligned in the name of press privilege. Whatever serves real people best must take priority over some cause or slogan" (Christians, 1983:112). By these terms, then, conveying the complete story about the Bhopal disaster, in the abstracted sense of journalists' search for truth, should not take precedence over the dignity of those involved in the process.

Based on these views, it would appear there probably was a "golden mean" of network television coverage of the Bhopal tragedy. Certainly, some pictures of the dead—and grieving— should have been shown. The massive number of dead and injured, and the human pain generated by the event, are an essential and compelling part of the story. To omit them entirely would have been to lie in a fundamental sense, to deprive those who saw the broadcasts not only of the abstract truth of the event but of some emotional recognition of the costs of the disaster.

Yet it also appears there is a case for saying the networks invaded the privacy of those most immediately involved in the event past rational justification. While carefully selected and judiciously culled footage of the innocent victims may have contributed to the overall truthfulness of the coverage, the repeated focus on burial and grief and the lack of discussion of long-term issues was in some sense the exploitation of innocent victims of a tragedy. This singular focus robbed Indians of their dignity as human beings and also may contribute to an uneasiness about the media and journalistic ethics in this country.

Taken on this level, the ethical discussion of the Bhopal coverage seems to argue for neither a prohibition of airing certain sorts of footage nor a complete sanction of it. Rather, journalistic restraint, buttressed by a commitment to all aspects of the story, would seem to benefit all involved.

THE NEED FOR PUBLIC ACTION

While the foregoing discussion concludes on the need for journalistic restraint, it also begs a central issue about Bhopal and other similar events. Ethical analysis of invasion of privacy generally has considered the impact of media attention on a single human being involved in an incident in which relatively few deaths or injuries are recorded. When the discussion shifts from this sort of incident to reportage of events in which hundreds or thousands of people may be killed or injured, then journalistic restraint—sometimes at the expense of truth—seems to be the norm. Scholarly studies conducted in the 1970s, for example, found that Ohio radio reporters tended to withhold some of the more alarming facts about possible tornadoes or urban disasters for fear of panicking listeners (Kueneman and Wright, 1975). Other studies found the media tend to deflate rather than inflate the number of dead and injured, as well as the amount of property damage, instead of "sensationalizing" such events (Scanlon et al., 1978). No doubt some of the impetus for such discretion arises from analyses of media coverage of the urban riots of the 1960s, when prestigious groups such as the Kerner Commission criticized the media for inflammatory reports.

However, for that group of scholars concerned with hazard mitigation—that is, preventing massive deaths and injuries as the result of natural and technological hazards—journalistic restraint raises a different set of questions. Hazards research has documented a phenomenon media scholars have only now begun to acknowledge: Despite reporters' and editors' perceptions, panic is a rare response (Mileti et al., 1975). Psychologists who study risk behavior analysis have concluded that most people, probably as a coping mechanism, have little idea of the nature and immediacy of the various risks associated with daily life, for example, wearing a seat belt, decreasing one's intake of fatty foods or building nuclear power plants near known earthquake faults.[7] Those people whose perceptions of risk are accurate are generally labeled clinically depressed, perhaps with good reason. Thus hazards scholars, and those in local, state and federal government whose job it is to plan for and deal with hazards, find they are unable to frame warning messages that will encourage the majority of those in danger to save their own lives (Ledingham and Masel-Walters, 1985).

The question becomes even more problematic when a technological hazard—for example, the construction of a chemical plant such as the one in Bhopal—becomes the core of the debate. The risks associated with such a facility—as well as the short-term trade-offs between employment and economic security versus long-term environmental safety and personal health—create a mind–boggling series of problems for scientists and scholars involved in the issue, as well as those who must cover it. Journalists, if the scholarly studies are correct, generally seem to err on the side of caution.

For example, scholarly studies of media reportage about Three Mile Island found that the media did not paint an accurately alarming portrait of what was happening inside the power plant, despite the fact that various experts employed by Metropolitan Edison and the Nuclear Regulatory Commission knew a partial meltdown had occurred (Friedman, 1981; Stephens and Edison, 1982).

Considering these documented tendencies, the ethical quandary for working journalists becomes more complex. On the one hand, there are the already acknowledged constraints concerning invasion of privacy and stereotyping which would seem to argue for continuing journalistic restraint. On the other hand, there is a growing body of social science literature, as well as a series of societal horror stories such as the Bhopal disaster or the coverage of the toxic chemical dioxin (Trost, 1984), which indicate the media have acted as something other than a "watchdog." Reporting primarily a cautious view of such events may, over time, blunt the edge of political and social debate. In the case of dioxin, it may also be argued that such cautious coverage actually cost lives.

These almost poetic descriptions reflected the second set of challenges that faced the journalists covering Bhopal. While the magnitude of the death and injury was great, the real story was that the leak itself is what has been described as a "normal accident" (Perrow, 1984). A normal accident, a term developed by a Harvard sociologist, is the sort of accident that can be expected—even predicted—to occur in many complex, highly sophisticated technological industries. Modern society has many examples of normal accidents: Three Mile Island, the Challenger explosion, the Soviet nuclear disaster and the chemical leak in Bhopal. In fact, accidents like the one in Bhopal are so normal that, according to government reports, more than 1,000 Americans have been injured in various forms of chemical accidents since 1980—and 135 of those injured died as a result.[5]

The issue here, thus, was getting the story behind the story. It was, in some sense, the task of reporting on the various values that science and technology, as expressed through the corporate world and through national governments, take on in the larger society. How these values are expressed, in turn, is a legitimate area for political debate. The deaths in Bhopal brought the world face to face with the "down side" of the economic and political expression of those values. However, it was the media's job to translate the images of death into their more global context. Scientists themselves, as well as media scholars, have argued:

—that a dialogue between public values and the scientific community establishes the process by which lay readers eventually start to become informed about science. Persons become interested in learning about science . . . once they perceive that the public has a mediating voice in establishing science policy.
—more discussion of popular values creates both a therapeutic social dialogue about science and contributes to a better under-

standing of science. "The important thing . . . is to give people a chance to argue, to interact and to make explicit the basis on which they prefer or reject each proposal" (Logan, 1985:57).

Almost all the print media analyzed made the connection, although it was weak in many instances. However, of all that was printed and broadcast in the first two months after the leak, 8.7 percent used Bhopal as a news peg to focus primarily on the issues surrounding technological hazards. Those same issues provided a secondary focus in an additional 7.0 percent of what was printed and aired, and they were mentioned tangentially in an additional 9.5 percent of the stories. Television, however, did not do nearly as well, for 90.2 percent of what it broadcast did not even mention the larger issues created by technological hazards, and only one television story (during the study period) focused directly on the issue.

The media also may have a more positive duty: a duty to save lives through enhanced social dialogue. When the issue becomes Bhopal or the lingering effects of dioxin in the biosphere, people can no longer be regarded exclusively as individuals. They are also members of a society that needs to make collective choices. As such the dead and the dying come to symbolize a societal struggle with the fruits of technology. Symbols have no circles of intimacy.

Ethicists have eschewed treating individuals as abstractions, rightly arguing that people are individuals and deserve the dignity accorded that distinction. In that vein, media ethicists have condemned the exploitation of the grief and suffering of innocent victims of tragedy.

Bhopal does not present such a case. While the death and injuries resulting from the leak are individual tragedies, they are also societal tragedies—the result of conscious choices by policy makers in both the economic and political spheres. Television, in the sense that it provided viewers with an intimate view of the result of those choices, provided responsible reportage of the event. It was reporting which, at least on the symbolic level, was capable of and did evoke an empathetic response from viewers. That response, in some cases, caused people to ask how they could prevent such a tragedy "at home." Out of such questions is social dialogue built.

However, the media's responsibility does not end with reporting merely the events. Both print and television journalists, and particularly broadcasters, need to begin framing the issue of technological hazards in a longer-term and more global context. Victims are profound symbols of what can happen with a technology gone wrong; but they do not symbolize the debate in which a democratic society needs to engage to decide what technologies, for what purposes, constitute acceptable risks. That debate is a journalistic story of first magnitude—and one which is not well served by relying exclusively on portraits of victims to make an important point. Reporters, be they political writers covering legislatures or business writers covering corporations, as well as those whose job it is to report science, need to begin a systematic job of educating themselves both to the ramifications of the debate and to the social and ethical values which underlie it. Then they need to transmit that value-oriented coverage to their readers and viewers.

Instead of waiting for the events as illustrations, journalists need to report questions about scientific and technological advance in the societal and political terms in which they ultimately will be decided. Such coverage requires a different conceptualization of news, one which includes ethical frames as a legitimate mode of analysis. Those ethical frames, in turn, need to be used in evaluative and analytical stories focusing on long-term and short-term questions of health, environmental safety and economics. It was the sort of coverage at which repeated viewing of Bhopal's victims hinted. But society needs more than hints. Journalism has a compelling ethical duty to provide information about "normal accidents" framed in ethical terms. Only then can democracies begin a much–needed, wide-ranging social and political debate on the fundamental questions science and technology now raise.

NOTES

1. I am indebted to my colleague Professor Robert Lester, Department of Religious Studies at the University of Colorado, for this cogent

explanation. His insights, both as a scholar and as someone who has lived in India, are greatly appreciated.

2. John S. Lang, "India's Tragedy—A Warning Heard Around the World," *U.S. News and World Report*, December 17, 1984, p. 25.

3. Pico Iyer (reported by Dean Brelis), "India's Nights of Death; More than 2,500 People Are Killed in the Worst Industrial Accident Ever," *Time*, December 17, 1984, p. 22.

4. Roger Rosenblat, "All the World Gasped; A tragic gas leak offers a parable of industrial life," *Time*, December 17, 1984, p. 20.

5. United Press International, "Toxic," October 3, 1985.

6. Numerous media ethics texts include case studies focusing on a journalistic invasion of shock and grief. However, it should be noted that television coverage of the August chemical leak in Institute—in which more than 100 persons were injured but no one died—was considerably more restrained.

7. Based on a statistical analysis, it is many times more "risky" to refuse to wear a seat belt than to live near the Diablo Canyon Nuclear Power Plant. The risks of a high-fat diet lie somewhere in between.

8

Shared Vulnerability

HASN'T IT ALWAYS BEEN THIS WAY?

The research reported in this book was based on one premise: Bhopal is the sort of story no journalist truly wants to write. While the public may still view journalists as reincarnations of *Front Page* protagonist Hildy Johnson, few contemporary journalists are willing to do anything for a story. Even fewer roar with triumph when disaster strikes, knowing that human suffering will bring them something so meaningless as a series of front-page by-lines or precious airtime on the network news. In this sense, the journalist is no different from the people he or she may cover; no one wants chemical spills that kill and injure thousands.

Such a frame of reference puts much of the research reported here into context. Journalists, as reporters and editors and as human beings who must confront catastrophe, report such events according to very traditional standards. Much of what the public reads and sees therefore becomes episodic, disconnected from human historical and cultural context. The accident in Bhopal is, only tangentially, connected to the accident in Insitute or to the literally thousands of chemical spills reported in the developing as well as the developed world. Journalists covered Bhopal in essentially the same way they would cover a congressional debate—or a city council meeting. They picked sides, quoted authoritative sources and remained objective about the larger issues of legal and political culpability. What was happening "right now" became the most important element of the story; discussion of long-range issues was relegated to the bottom of the page, or to lengthy analysis and investigative pieces which only the determined reader or viewer would complete. Television did what it has always done well, bringing its audience face-to-face with the suffering the tragedy caused as well as providing updates of events. But television stuck only to what it does well. The broadcast medium, without any type of formal collusion among the networks, omitted discussion of almost everything that was long-term and many-faceted about Bhopal. The event itself became the only story the medium believed was worth reporting.

The patterns of power created by such reporting were largely institutional in nature, focusing as they did on existing governments and corporations. Individual citizens, their views and their fears, were background to the larger, event-oriented story. Scientists and doctors, who could have added layers of complexity to the debate, figured less prominently in the public discourse. Science, because it tends not to have firm answers to questions such as "will this leak cause cancer" does not fit well into a debate—for science is almost always equivocal on such issues. In such an artificial environment, helplessness becomes a prominent theme, for the Indians themselves were obviously helpless when it came to a gas leak in the middle of the night. Government and corporate officials could only react; the fact that such an event could have been anticipated both by governments and by Union Carbide—as well as those citizens who chose to become informed on the issue—was a point of view that was never clearly connected to the tragedy.

In some sense, the journalists covering Bhopal became the victims of their own, limited definitions of what constitutes news. A single episode in human history, pried from its cultural, historic and scientific context, was what the media reported. There is little that is factually incorrect about such coverage, and it adhered to traditional standards of news judgment and newsworthiness. What is wrong falls more into the category of what was omitted: the history of a country which has had to struggle to feed itself, the debate over planning for technological modernization, the scientific understanding of the needs for and costs of agricultural production boosted by chemical means.

The broad outline of what was conveyed, at least six months after the event, was firmly entrenched in the public memory. That fact is perhaps the most remarkable finding of this study, for, if past research were to provide the only indication, then people should have remembered little about the events in Bhopal. Some, of course, did remember little. But journalists and hazards scholars need to know that much of what the media said did "get through" and was retained by those who watched and read it.

People retained not only facts—sometimes the incorrect facts—but vivid visual impressions. What they said they remembered of Bhopal was the dead and the dying, and sometimes the potential for later death, as it was presented vividly on television and less graphically but still powerfully in the print media. Moreover, those memories were influenced; people who perceived exposure to chemical hazards as part of their daily lives remembered more, remembered more "correct" facts and recalled what they had read and seen more vividly. These people used media for something vital in their lives: to help them attempt to gain a sense of psychological security through the type of environmental surveillance that only the media—in this information age—can provide.

Such surveillance, propelled as it is by a basic psychological need that all human beings possess, is subject to nuance. But those nuances of events in Bhopal, and the various decisions and events which contributed to it, were most often missing in media reports. Instead, the media brought a more mythical structure to the events in Bhopal. The media portrayed the risks of the accident as if they were involuntary, delayed, unknown, uncontrollable, unfamiliar, dreaded, catastrophic and fatal (Slovic, 1980).

Such a constellation of traits helps to produce, or may reinforce, the helpless reaction that many of those interviewed expressed. Such a view takes on a mythical structure which has a profound counterpoint to play in the existing American character. For Americans believe, simultaneously, that democratic government represents the people and that the average person has little to say about governmental decisions. Americans believe they can fight city hall; but once they get there, they believe government officials are almost invincible—and, perhaps worse, that individual citizens are only infrequently capable of understanding and thereby influencing what government does.

Thus is the interaction of media reports, myth and belief born, recreating the famous "pseudo-event" of which Lippmann (1949) spoke. Bhopal was portrayed as the kind of event people most dread, with little context and with certain essential facts omitted. Should people choose to believe such an analysis, one which is the creature of traditional definitions of news just as much as any particular set of facts, they may decide to take themselves out of the political debates which make Bhopal and other sorts of normal accidents possible. Some will be galvanized by what they see and read, but others will decide the forces and the task arrayed against them are simply too strong to overcome. They will leave the debate to the experts who may not only have different goals and desires from the average citizen but also who, at least if Bhopal is any indication, are just as capable of making mistakes as the average American or Indian may be.

If that is the case, then there may be more Bhopal stories for journalists to write, more corpses, more injuries, more "normal" accidents that are the result of conscious political and economic choices. But it does not have to be that way. If I am correct, if journalists do not relish writing such stories, and if journalists believe that one of the goals of their profession is to spur societal debate, then there are things that can be done. These efforts will require journalists to work a little harder, but they are efforts which may ultimately serve the larger goals of democratic discourse to which the profession adheres.

PLAN FOR CHANGE

In one sense, if journalists are to do a better job reporting on technological hazards and normal accidents, what they need to do is nothing less than reexamine the values of their own profession. Luckily for those working in the field, much of that reexamination already has been done, by groups such as the British Commission on the Press and by the Hutchins Commission. The recommendations of those two commissions are, by now, well–known and somewhat accepted, at least in scholarly circles and in some newsrooms as well. But, in another sense, if journalists are to do a better job covering the complex issues hazards raise, they need merely to alter some of their daily habits and to become recommitted to getting "the story behind the story . . . the in-depth angle . . . complete and comprehensive coverage." Such a commitment is not lacking within the profession; what remains is to actualize it in certain situations. Thus, if journalists are to remedy some of their own shortcomings, I suggest the following four-point program.

One: Provide a context for the event. While initial reports of disaster, be they hurricanes or nuclear power accidents, will be largely event–centered, it is possible, even early in the coverage, to place the events in larger context. It is not enough to say that Bhopal is the most severe chemical disaster in human history. It is more sufficient to report that a certain number of similar accidents have happened, both in the United States and in other countries, and to place the Bhopal event in perspective. It would be better still if the Bhopal event could be framed in the larger issues which surrounded the plant—the need for jobs in the developing world, the need for food in those same countries and the role that chemical pesticides and fertilizers play in fulfilling these national and human needs. Not all stories, of course, could do this. But many of them could, and the broadcast medium is just as capable of providing this kind of context as are the print media.

Two: Provide a discussion of the science of the event. Journalists particularly need to abandon the notion of lining various experts up on two sides of a question and letting them "have at" each other and their opposing points of view. Science is seldom so clear. What journalists need to do is to find experts and quote them, explaining clearly to readers and viewers that the answers science may provide are neither all-inclusive nor unilateral. This approach, in turn, means that journalists themselves are going to have to become better informed about science and less concerned about printing and broadcasting stories which follow a neat formula or lend themselves to a snappy "close."

In this sense, journalists need to give their readers and viewers a little intellectual credit while acknowledging that a more sophisticated and multiperspective presentation of the news will "miss" some readers and viewers. Yet many of those who said they remembered something of the Bhopal coverage indicated, in various ways, that they could have understood more, and, in many cases, had questions the media reports had not answered. It seems more than appropriate, at this stage of mass communication development, that some stories about significant events seek not just the lowest common denominator but strive to match a rather sophisticated reader or viewer "need to know" with equally sophisticated reporting.

When readers and viewers tell journalists there are questions that remain unanswered, that they are able to perceive patterns to events and to relate events and issues to their own lives, then it is time for journalists to provide more—not less—information. Such information should, in turn, emphasize underlying issues and underlying contexts. It should be unafraid to tell readers and viewers that there are questions that remain to be both asked and answered. Certainly one of the most important of these questions is the trade-off society makes between long- and short-term risks.

Such a presentation would require a different form of reporting—one which blends analysis based on an ethical approach to the discussion of various "goods" for society and individuals with more traditional fact gathering. However, corporate officials, government agencies and those who work for them, and individual human beings who make decisions daily about how they will live their lives and feed themselves and their families are performing such an analysis. It seems absurd that the mass media could not at least aid that effort.

Three: Broaden and significantly alter existing sourcing patterns. Scientists and science writers have long complained that, on stories which include at least some aspect of science, they are seldom consulted by the mass media. This approach, particularly to coverage of technological hazards, needs to change— and it is journalists who need to do most of the changing. In-depth reportage of such events would demand that journalists become more educated about the scientific aspects of these various stories, and that they seek out and quote scientific experts even if what those experts say does not fit neatly into a two-sided dialogue.

At the same time, the "experts" need to understand that the mass media, because their central role is to translate largely technical and complex knowledge for wide dissemination, will ask "simple" questions and often expect too-easy answers. Scientists are often coy and rather easily frustrated when dealing with journalists; mutual communication in this sense will require the development of trust on which each side will have "to give a little."

Those whose primary concern has been hazard mitigation need to realize that for them to achieve their goals, involvement with the mass media—in the best sense of the word—is fundamental. Journalists, on the other hand, need to make these overtures and changes without abandoning the traditional journalist stance of questioning what they are told and refusing to accept "expert" statements strictly at face value. If Bhopal does nothing else, it provides ample evidence that experts—be they corporate or governmental—can make mistakes. Journalists need to remember this lesson from Bhopal, too.

Four: Shift, through inclusion of context and discussion of long-term issues, the tone of news reports. Hazards, particularly technological hazards, can be placed within the network of political and social debate which characterize democratic decision making. By providing readers and viewers with a more complete story, and by allowing those who are willing and able to bring a sophisticated understanding of some parts of that story into focus through media reports, individual citizens will begin to understand that they have some power to make decisions about the risks society takes and some compelling reasons for doing so. Different individuals, of course, will be involved at different levels; some will choose not to be involved. But, in a democracy, not everyone has to be involved to make a change in policy choices or to bring previously unconsidered alternatives to the fore.

In this sense, knowledge wrapped in a historic, scientific, and issue-centered meaning is empowering. It tells people that there are things they can do to mitigate the impact of hazards in their lives. Further, it gives them some sense of the trade-offs they make; the costs of the risks they are willing to take. Journalists do not have to advocate such activity in their news reporting. But it is equally "one-sided and unobjective" to report the news in such a way as to suggest that such activity is not possible, or is futile, or that it can be undertaken only by governments acting in their own interests or by corporations acting primarily for porfit.

Reportage of technological hazards such as Bhopal, in this sense, needs to place the issue in the context of the political, social and economic debates which gave rise to it in the first place. In a democracy, however, the hazards debate is one in which individuals should have a say. Comprehensive media reports can provide information to encourage such discourse as well as providing a more subtle tone that suggests such discourse is both appropriate and capable of leading to change.

THE SHARED VULNERABILITY OF BHOPAL

In the final analysis, the essential story that the media need to present—and which the community of hazards scholars needs to affirm—is that we are all vulnerable to accidents such as the one in Bhopal. By the nature of much foreign news coverage, Americans are often shielded from such an understanding. Bhopal, and the more recent Soviet nuclear accident at Chernobyl, are changing that awareness. Some of that change is due, at least in part, to a mass media which brought the story of these disasters "home." But, in bringing that message to our doorsteps, the media, and those of us who consume it, need to be aware that such catastrophes are not myth; they are man-made and they can be mitigated. Shared vulnerability can mean that the next chemical, or nuclear, or industrial accident is just around the corner from each of us. However, because that vulnerability is something we share with the world, it also means it is something we have the power to change. Vulnerability does not equate with inevitability. It is the ramifications of vulnerability that the media need to present. Those whose work it is to mitigate the vulnerability that does exist need to insist the complete story be told.

Selected Bibliography

Arlen, Michael J. *Living Room War*. New York: Penguin Books, 1982.

Atkins, Charles. "Effects of Realistic TV Violence vs Fictional Violence on Aggression," *Journalism Quarterly*, 60:615–612, Winter 1983.

Atwater, Tony, Salwen, Michael B., and Anderson, Ronald. "Media Agenda Setting with Environmental Issues," *Journalism Quarterly*, 62(2):393–397, 1985.

Belman, Lary S. "John Dewey's Concept of Communication," *Journal of Communication*, 27(1):29–37, 1977.

Bledsoe, Robert L., Headberg, Roger, Maddox, William I., Lenon, David R., and Long, Dennis A. "Foreign Affairs Coverage in Elite and Mass Periodicals," *Journalism Quarterly*, 59:471–474, Autumn 1982.

Browne, Karen. "Comparison of Factual Recall from Film–Print Stimuli," *Journalism Quarterly*, 55:350–353, Summer 1978.

Budd, Ricard W., Thorp, Robert K., and Donohew, Lewis. *Content Analysis of Communications*. New York: Macmillan, 1967.

Burton, Ian, Victor, Peter, and Whyte, Anne, eds. *The Mississauga Evacuation: Final Report*. Toronto: Institute for Environmental Studies, University of Toronto, 1981.

Burton, Ian, Kates, Robert W., and White, Gilbert F. *The Environment as Hazard*. New York: Oxford University Press, 1978.

Carey, James W. "A Cultural Approach to Communication," *Communication*, 2:1–22, 1975.

Christians, Clifford G., Rotzoll, Kim B., and Fackler, Mark. *Media Ethics, Cases and Moral Reasoning*. New York: Longman, 1983.

Clark, John R., Carter, T. Michael, and Leik, Robert K. "Organizational and Household Response to Hurricane Warnings in the Local

Community." Paper presented to the Annual Meetings of the American Association for the Advancement of Science, Houston, 1979.

Cole, Bruce J. "Trends in Science and Conflict Coverage in Four Metropolitan Newspapers," *Journalism Quarterly*, 52:465–471, Autumn 1975.

Combs, Barbara, and Slovic, Paul. "Newspaper Coverage of Causes of Death," *Journalism Quarterly*, 56(4):837–843, 849.

Cronholm, Margareta, and Sandall, Rolf. "Scientific Information: A Review of Research," *Journal of Communication*, 31(2):85–96, 1981.

Culbert, David. "Historians and the Visual Analysis of Television News," in *Television Network News*, Wiliam Adams and Fay Schreibman, eds. Washington D.C.: George Washington University Press, 1978, pp. 139–151.

Dangerheld, Linda A., McCartney, Hunter P., and Starcher, Ann T. "How Did Mass Communication, as Sentry, Perform in the Gasoline Crunch," *Journalism Quarterly*, 52:316–320, Summer 1975.

Davies, James C. *Human Nature in Politics*. New York: John Wiley & Sons, 1963.

Deutchmann, Paul J., and Danielson, Wayne A. "Diffusion of Knowledge of a Major News Story," *Journalism Quarterly*, 37(3):345–355, Summer 1960.

Drabeck, Thomas E., and Quarantelli, Enrico L. "Scapegoats, Villains, and Disasters," *Trans-action*, 4 (March):12–17, 1967.

Elliott, William R., and Schenck-Hamlin, William J. "Film, Politics and the Press: The Influence of All the President's Men," *Journalism Quarterly*, 56(3):546–553, Autumn 1979.

Engler, Robert. "Many Bhopals: Technology Out of Control," *The Nation*, April 27, 1985, pp. 488–500.

Frank, Robert S. "The Grammar of Film in Television News," *Journalism Quarterly*, 51(2):254–251, Summer 1974.

Friedman, Sharon, M. "Blueprint for Breakdown: Three Mile Island and the Media Before the Accident," *Journal of Communication*, 31(2):116–128, Spring 1981.

Friemuth, Vicki S., and VanNevel, J. Paul. "Reaching the Public: The Asbestos Awareness Campaign," *Journal of Communication*, 31(2):155–167, Spring 1981.

Gans, Herbert J. *Deciding What's News*. New York: Vintage, 1979.

Gantz, Walter. "How Uses and Gratifications Affect Recall of Television News," *Journalism Quarterly*, 55(4):664–672, Winter 1978.

Gerbner, George. "Press Perspectives in World Communication," *Journalism Quarterly*, 38(3):313–322, Summer 1961.

Gerbner, George, and Marvanyi, George. "The Many Worlds of the World's Press," *Journal of Communication*, 27(1):52–66, Winter 1977.

Gerbner, George, and Signorielli, Helen. "The World of Television News," in *Television Network News*, William Adams and Fay Schreibman, eds. Washington D.C.: George Washington University Press, 1978, pp. 189–196.

Hiroi, Osamu, Mikami, Shunji, and Miyata, Kakuko. "A Study of Mass Media Reporting in Emergencies," *International Journal of Mass Emergencies and Disasters*, 3(1):21–49, 1985.

Hodges, Louis W. "The Journalist and Privacy," *Social Responsibility: Journalism, Law and Medicine*. Lexington, Va.: Washington & Lee University, 9 (1983):11–23.

Hofstetter, C. Richard, Zukin, Cliff, and Buss, Terry F. "Political Imagery and Information in an Age of Television," *Journalism Quarterly*, 55(3):562–569, Autumn 1978.

Hungerford, Stephen E., and Lemert, James B. "Covering the Environment: A New Afghanistanism," *Journalism Quarterly*, 50:3, Spring 1973.

Katz, Elihu, Blumler, Jay G., and Gurevitch, Michael. "Utilization of Mass Communication by the Individual," in *The Uses of Mass Communications: Current Perspectives on Gratifications Research*, Jay G. Blumler and Elihu Katz, eds., Beverly Hills: Sage, 1974, pp. 19–32.

Keller, Edward B. "The Flap Over Plutonium: An Element of Risk," *Journal of Communication*, 29(3):54–61, Summer 1979.

Knight, Graham, and Dean, Tony. "Myth and the Structure of News," *Journal of Communication*, 32(3):144–161, Spring 1982.

Kraus, Sidney, Davis, Dennis, Lang, Gladys Engel, and Lang, Kurt. "Critical Events Analysis," in *Political Communication*, Steven H. Chaffee, ed. Beverly Hills: Sage, 1975, pp. 195–216.

Krieghbaum, Hillier. "Three Mile Island Coverage: A Crash Course for Readers," *Mass Communication Review*, 6(2):2–10, Spring 1979.

Kueneman, Rodney M., and Wright, Joseph E. "News Policies of Broadcast Stations for Civil Disturbances and Disasters," *Journalism Quarterly*, 52(4):670–677, Winter 1975.

Larson, James F. "International Affairs Coverage on U.S. Network Television," *Journal of Communication*, 29(2):136–147, Spring 1979.

Lasswell, Harold D. "The Structure and Function of Communication," in *The Communication of Ideas*, L. Bryson, ed. New York: Harper and Row, 1958.

Ledingham, John A., and Masel-Walters, Lynne. "Written on the Wind:

The Media and Hurricane Alicia," *Newspaper Research Journal*, 6(2):50–58, Winter 1985.

Lee, Raymond S. H. "Credibility of Newspaper and Television News," *Journalism Quarterly*, 55(2):282–287, Summer 1978.

Lent, John A. "Foreign News in American Media," *Journal of Communication*, 27(1):46–51, 1977.

Lepkowski, Wil. "Bhopal: City Struggling for Normalcy a Year After Disaster," *Chemical and Engineering News*, December 2, 1985, pp. 18–32.

————. "Chemical Safety in Developing Countries: the Lessons of Bhopal," *Chemical and Engineering News*, April 8, 1985, pp. 9–14.

————. "Bhopal: The Continuing Story," *Chemical and Engineering News*, February 11, 1985, pp. 3–65.

Levine, Grace Ferrari. "Learned Helplessness and the Evening News," *Journal of Communication*, 27(4):100–105, 1977.

Lichty, Lawrence W., and Bailey, George A. "Reading the Wind: Reflections on Content Analysis of Broadcast News," in *Television Network News*, William Adams and Fay Schreibman, eds. Washington D.C.: George Washington University Press, 1978, pp. 111–138.

Lifton, Robert Jay. *Death in Life*. New York: Simon and Schuster, 1967.

Lifton, Robert Jay, and Falk, Richard. *Indefensible Weapons*. New York: Basic Books, 1982.

Lippmann, Walter. *Public Opinion*. New York: The Free Press, 1949.

Logan, Robert A. "Commentary: Rationales for Investigative and Explanatory Trends in Science Reporting," *Newspaper Research Journal*, 7(1):53–58, 1985.

McCombs, Maxwell E., and Shaw, Donald. "The Agenda–Setting Function of the Mass Media," *Public Opinion Quarterly*, 36:176–187, 1972.

McGuire, William J. "Psychological Motives and Communication Gratification," in *The Uses of Mass Communications*, Jay G. Blumler and Elihu Katz, eds. Beverly Hills: Sage, 1974, pp. 167–198.

McKay, Jennifer M. "Newspaper Reporting of Bushfire Disaster in Southeastern Australia—Ash Wednesday, 1983," *Disasters*, 7(4):1–8, 1984.

McKay, Jennifer M., and Finlayson, Brian. "Observations on Mass Media Reporting and Individual Motivation to Obtain a Flood Inundation Map—River Torrents, Adelaide, South Australia," *Applied Geography*, 1982, pp. 143–153.

McQuail, Denis. *Mass Communication Theory*. Beverly Hills: Sage, 1983.

Malaney, Gary D., Buss, Terry F. "AP Wire Reports vs CBS-Television

News Coverage of the Presidential Campaign," *Journalism Quarterly*, 56:602–610, Autumn 1979.

Malinowski, Bronislaw. *Myth in Primitive Psychology*. New York: Negro Universities Press, 1974.

Maslow, Abraham H. *Motivation and Personality*. New York: Harper and Row, 1954.

Mazur, Allan. "Media Coverage and Public Opinion on Scientific Controversies," *Journal of Communication*, 31(2):106–115, Spring 1981.

Mileti, Dennis S., Drabek, Thomas E., and Hass, J. Eugene. *Human Systems in Extreme Environments, A Sociological Perspective*. Boulder, Colo.: Institute for Behavioral Science, 1975.

Miller, Jon D., and Barrington, Thomas M. "The Acquisition and Retention of Scientific Information," *Journal of Communication*, 31(2):178–189, Spring 1981.

Mujahid, Sharifial. "Coverage of Pakistan in Three U.S. Newsmagazines," *Journalism Quarterly*, 47(1):126–130, Spring 1970.

Needham, R. D. and Nelson, J. G. "Newspaper Response to Flood and Erosion Hazards on the North Lake Erie Shore," *Environmental Management*, 1(6):521–540, 1977.

Nielsen, Richard P., and Nielsen, Angela F. "Communications and Fatalism," *Journalism Quarterly*, 51(1):713–720, Spring 1974.

Nigg, Joanne M. "Communication Under Conditions of Uncertainty: Understanding Earthquake Forecasting," *Journal of Communication*, 32(1):27–36, Winter 1982.

Nimmo, Dan. "TV Network News Coverage of Three Mile Island: Reporting Disasters as Technological Fables," *International Journal of Mass Emergencies and Disasters* 2 (March):115–145, 1984.

Novici, Kenneth, and Sandman, Peter M. "How Use of Mass Media Affect Views on Solutions to Environmental Problems," *Journalism Quarterly*, 51(3):448–452, Autumn 1974.

O'Keefe, Garrett J. "Political Malaise and Reliance on Media," *Journalism Quarterly*, 57:122–128, Spring 1980.

Park, R. E. "News and a Form of Knowledge," *American Journal of Sociology*, 45:669–686, 1940.

Patterson, Thomas E. "Assessing Television Newscasts: Future Directions in Content Analysis," in *Television Network News*, William Adams and Fay Schreibman, eds. Washington D.C.: George Washington University Press, 1978, pp. 177–187.

———. *The Mass Media Election*. New York: Praeger, 1980.

Perrow, Charles. *Normal Accidents: Living With High–Risk Technologies*. New York: Basic Books, 1984.

Quarantelli, E. L. "The Command Post Point of View in Local Mass

Communications Systems," *Communication: International Journal of Communication Research* 7(1981):57–73.

Reser, J. P. "The Psychological Reality of Natural Disasters," in *Response to Disaster*, Oliver, J., ed. Centre of Disaster Studies, James Cook University of North Queensland, 1980, pp. 29–44.

Rich, Jonathan T. "A Measure of Comprehensiveness in Newsmagazine Science Coverage," *Journalism Quarterly*, 58(2):248–253, Summer 1981.

Riebsame, William E. "News Media Coverage of Seasonal Forecasts: The Case of Winter 1982–1983," *Bulletin of American Meteorological Society*, 64(12):1351–1356, 1983.

Roberts, Churchill. "The Presentation of Blacks in Television Network News," *Journalism Quarterly*, 52(1):50–55, Spring 1975.

Robinson, John P. "World Affairs Information and Mass Media Exposure," *Journalism Quarterly* 44(1):23–31, Spring 1967.

Robinson, Michael, and Sheehan, Gail. *Over the Wire and On TV*. New York: Basic Books, 1984.

Rogers, Everett M., and Sood, Rahul. "Mass Media Operations in a Quick Onset Natural Disaster: Hurricane David in Dominica." Boulder, Colo.: Institute for Behavioral Science, Natural Hazards Research Working Paper #41, 1981.

Rubin, Alan M. "A Multivariate Analysis of 60 Minutes Viewing Motivations," *Journalism Quarterly*, 58:529–533, Winter 1981.

Saarinen, Thomas E. *Perspectives on Increasing Hazard Awareness*. Boulder, Colo.: Institute for Behavioral Science, Program on Environment and Behavior Monograph #35, 1982.

Salcedo, Rodolfo N., Halley, Read, Evans, James F., and Kong, Ana C. "A Successful Information Campaign on Pesticide," *Journalism Quarterly* 51(1):91–96, Spring 1974.

Scanlon, T. Joseph, Luukka, Rodu, and Morton, Gerald. "Media Coverage of a Crisis: Better than Reported, Worse than Necessary," *Journalism Quarterly*, 55(1):68–72, 1978.

Seligman, M. E. P. *Helplessness*. San Francisco: W. H. Freeman, 1975.

Slovic, Paul, Baruch, Fischhoff, and Lichtenstein, Sarah. "Facts and Fears: Understanding Perceived Risk," R. C. Shwing and W. Al Albers, eds. *Societal Risk Assessment: How Safe Is Safe Enough?* New York: Plenum, 1980.

Smith, Robert Rutherford. "Mythic Elements in Television News," *Journal of Communication*, 29 (1):75–84, 1979.

Snyder, Louis L., and Morris, Richard B., ed. *A Treasury of Great Reporting*. New York: Simon and Schuster, 1962.

Sood, Rahul. "Communicating for Improved Hazard Awareness," in

Perspectives on Increasing Hazard Awareness, Thomas E. Saarinen, ed. Boulder, Colo.: Institute for Behavioral Science, Program on Environment and Behavior Monograph #35, 1982, pp. 97–129.

Sorensen, John H. "Emergency to Mount St. Helens' Eruption: March 20 to April 10, 1980," Boulder, Colo.: Institute for Behavioral Science, Hazard Research Working Paper #43, 1982.

———. "Knowing How to Behave Under the Threat of Disaster," *Environment and Behavior*, 15(4):438–457, 1983.

Stephens, Mitchell, and Edison, Nadyne G. "Coverage of Events at Three Mile Island," *Mass Communication Review*, 7(3):3–9, Fall 1980.

———. "News Media Coverage of Issues During the Accident at Three-Mile Island," *Journalism Quarterly*, 59(2):199–204, Summer 1982.

Trost, Cathy. *Elements of Risk*. New York: Times Books, 1984.

Tuchman, G. "Making News by Doing Work: Routinizing the Unexpected," *American Journal of Sociology*, 79 (1973–74): 110–131.

Waxman, Jerry L. "Local Broadcast Gatekeeping During Natural Disasters," *Journalism Quarterly*, 30(4):751–58, Winter 1973.

Weaver, David H., and Wilhoit, G. Cleveland. "Foreign News Coverage in Two U.S. Wire Services," *Journal of Communication*, 31(2):55–63, Spring 1981.

Wenger, Dennis. "A Few Empirical Observations Concerning the Relationship Between the Mass Media and Disaster Knowledge: A Research Report," *Disasters and the Mass Media*. Washington D.C.: National Academy of Sciences, 1980.

Wilhoit, G. Cleveland, and Weaver, David. "Foreign News Coverage in Two U.S. Wire Services: An Update," *Journal of Communication*, 33(2):132–148, Spring 1983.

Wilkins, Lee. "Television and Newspaper Coverage of a Blizzard: Is the Message Helplessness?" *Newspaper Research Journal*, 6(4):51–65, 1985.

Winert, Richard A., Leckliter, Ingrid N., Chinn, Donna E., and Stahl, Brian. "Reducing Energy Consumption: The Long-term Effects of a Single Television Program," *Journal of Communication*, 34(3):37–51, Summer 1984. *Chemical Risks: Fears, Facts, and the Media*. Washington D.C.: The Media Institute, 1985.

Index

lines, 56; economic coverage, 57, 59–60; event-oriented coverage, 56–57, 61; helplessness, 109; Institute as focus, 58; long-term issues, 59; political coverage, 55, 58; portrayal of victims, 61; powerful actors, 106; predictive stories, 61; risk-benefit analysis, 57; sources, 97, 101–3; story subject, 57; technological hazard coverage, 57–59

Waxman, Henry, 9, 16, 17, 20, 21

Weaver, David, 29

Wenger, Dennis, 28

West Germany, 6

Wilhoit, G. Cleveland, 29

Wire service reports, 46–54; and blame, 51; cultural background, 52; datelines, 46; economic background, 52; geographic location of Bhopal, 48; helplessness, 109–10; mitigation coverage, 52–53; portrayal of victims, 50–51; sources, 99–101; technological hazard focus, 50. *See also* AP, Reuters, UPI.

Woodbine, Georgia, 6, 9, 10

Workers, role at Bhopal, 1, 3, 17, 20

World War I, 85, 91

Wright, Joseph, 31, 37, 141

Zukin, Cliff, 30

About the Author

LEE WILKINS earned her doctorate in political science and is Assistant Professor in the School of Journalism and Mass Communication at the University of Colorado, Boulder. She has contributed to *International Journal of Mass Emergencies and Disasters, Newspaper Research Journal, Political Psychology, Critical Studies in Mass Communication* and *Journal of Mass Media Ethics*. She is the author of *Wayne Morse: A Bio-Bibliography* (Greenwood Press, 1985).